UNBROKEN CIRCLE

HOW TO TAKE YOUR FAMILY THROUGH THE END TIME

W9-ABS-636

JOHN & MILLIE YOUNGBERG

Pacific Press Publishing Association
Nampa, Idaho
Oshawa, Ontario, Canada

Edited by Jerry D. Thomas
Cover photo by Richard Kaylin for Tony Stone Images
Cover and inside design by Dennis Ferree

Copyright ©1997 by
Pacific Press Publishing Association
Printed in the United States of America
All Rights Reserved

ISBN 0-8163-1344-X

97 98 99 00 01 • 5 4 3 2 1

This book is dedicated to
our children and grandchildren
and to all those who
"desire a better, that is, a heavenly country"
—who "seek a homeland."

CONTENTS

Introduction		9
Chapter 1	The Old Home Place	13
Chapter 2	The First Home	20
Chapter 3	He Made It!	27
Chapter 4	The Ark's Ready!	32
Chapter 5	A Woman's Drama	39
Chapter 6	Seeking a Homeland	43
Chapter 7	Going Home or Settling In?	51
Chapter 8	The Last Night of Sodom	60
Chapter 9	Trouble En Route	68
Chapter 10	Family Sealed by Blood	77
Chapter 11	Almost There	84
Chapter 12	How Far From Home?	92
Chapter 13	Skeleton in the Family Closet	101
Chapter 14	Bloodstained Choices	106
Chapter 15	The Bloodstained Path	112
Chapter 16	Coming Out of Babylon—Psychological Roadblocks	120
Chapter 17	Coming Out of Babylon—Material Roadblocks	132
Chapter 18	Coming Out of Babylon—Family Dynamics	143

Chapter 19	The Holy Spirit Draws Us Home	152
Chapter 20	Children Going Home	160
Chapter 21	The Great Controversy at the Family Level	173
Chapter 22	Your Family and the Scarlet Beast	186
Chapter 23	The Family's Last Call	193
Chapter 24	Don't They Want to Come Home?	204
Chapter 25	Traveling the Narrow Way	207
Chapter 26	Home at Last!	212

ACKNOWLEDGMENTS

The authors express appreciation to Winston Ferris for assistance in paraphrasing "Traveling the Narrow Way," to Matthias Müller and Ruzica Gregor for ideas on Lot and on archaeological references concerning Sodom, to William Taggart III for ideas in the chapter on "The Scarlet Beast," to G. Edward Reid for concepts about "God's Great Clock," to Yvonne Terry for editing the manuscript and adapting "Don't They Want to Come Home?," and to Kenneth Corkum for a critical reading of the manuscript. Many of the ideas in the book have been borrowed from Ellen White. In case of direct quote, we have tried to give the reference. We particularly thank George and Imogene Akers and Ina Mae and Oliver White—our partners in prayer—with whom we have often knelt in weakness and risen encouraged in the Spirit and strengthened for the task.

INTRODUCTION

A search of Scripture reveals only a few verses that deal theologically with the subject of the family and the last days. These include 1 Corinthians 7:29-31; Ephesians 5:25-27; 2 Timothy 3:1-4; Matthew 24: 37-39; Joel 2:28, 29; Malachi 4:5, 6—and that's about it. Because of our interest in both the family and eschatology, we have pondered much over this and have finally concluded that in inspiring Scripture, the Holy Spirit has chosen to deal with this subject largely through historical incidents, case studies, and illustrations. Though we feel we are living in the end time, certainly Noah and his family also lived in an end time. Thus by reviewing the accounts of his family—and of similar heroic families of faith who survived crises—we can learn much that is applicable to the last-day situation.

In the last few years, a battery of good books have been published on end-time events. They are a blessing to God's remnant people who expect to see Him coming soon in the clouds of heaven. However, these books make little reference to families in the last days. Some novels have portrayed families living in the end time. Though interesting, their purpose is not to deal with actual historical families or to rightly interpret Scripture. The absence of material in this area has added urgency to this writing and publication.

I remember preaching my first sermon on families in the last days. It was entitled "The Elijah Message." That was more than forty years ago. This has become a favorite theme of mine, and since then, Millie and I have gathered hundreds of pages of material on the subject. However, recently one of my doctoral students pointed out to me that the *Elijah* message is just one link in a basic Bible motif of *coming out.* This helped me to place the subject within a more adequate biblical context. Thus Noah was called to come out of a wicked generation and enter the ark, Abraham was called to come out of Mesopotamia, Lot was called to come out of Sodom, Israel was called out of Egypt, and Elijah on Mt. Carmel called Israel to come out of Baal worship and serve the true Lord. Since New Testament times, God has called out a church, the *ekklesia*, which literally means the "called out." Indeed, the whole Bible is a story of "coming out." Many of the "coming out" stories have significant family dimensions that have often eluded us.

The Elijah message is a Seventh-day Adventist term not commonly used by other Christians. Concretely, it refers to the message of Malachi 4:5, 6 and usually applies it directly to a family relationship call to turn the hearts of parents to children and children to their parents. It is not understood to mean that Elijah personally returns to earth but that before the second coming of Christ a work will be done in families to "prepare the way for the Lord" (Isaiah. 40:3-5) "in the spirit and power of Elijah" (Luke 1:17).

This book deals with the end-time scenario of *families coming out of Babylon*. However, instead of emphasizing the organizational dimensions of Babylon, it looks more into human experience and at the Babylon that beckons to all of us. This book considers the experiential dimension of Babylon. If Babylon were real estate, we could all arrange for

Introduction

transportation and escape. But if Babylon lurks in our hearts and lifestyle, then the central issue is not geographical or organizational. *The problem is not so much getting the family out of Babylon as it is getting Babylon out of the family.* The problem about heaven is not logistical. It is not how we can get a family from way down here to way up there. *It is not a problem of getting families into heaven but of getting heaven into families.* When the latter is accomplished, the former will take care of itself.

Some of these chapters have been written by Millie, some by John. We have different writing styles. In the early seminars we gave together, sometimes we would have serious disagreements over whether things should be done one way or another. Millie tends to be more creative, imaginative, and story-oriented. John leans toward the conceptual and the structured. However, in writing this book we have had no couple crisis! We have helped each other on the chapters and tried to complement each other. In gratitude to God for joining our lives twenty-five years ago, we have tried to enhance each other and give our readers the best of both our approaches.

The rough drafts on many of the chapters were written at our mountain hideaway in North Carolina by John, who was accompanied only by the squirrels, the nesting phoebe and her little ones, the pileated woodpecker, the scarlet tanager, the indigo bunting, and the friendly rabbit. In Millie's coming and going, she took charge of some of the most difficult chapters. When we returned to civilization, Yvonne Terry cut, modified, and substituted with editorial flurry. We thank her for improving the flow of the chapters.

How To Use *Unbroken Circle*
- Read it personally and reflect on the "For Your Family" activities.
- Read it personally and choose appropriate "For Your Family" activities to use for family worship.

- Read as a family for family worship and select appropriate "For Your Family" activities to enrich the worship experience. A chapter could be extended for a week or more as there is family interest. The chapters may be more applicable for youth, but with adaptation, they can be used with young children as well.
- Use in a small group fellowship where emphasis is given to prayer for the family.
- The material can also be used for sermons, prayer meetings, radio talk shows, or TV presentations—just give credit to the authors.

May God bless these humble lines and use them to His honor and glory to make the way just a little clearer, happier, and encouraging for you and your family. May you find heaven with an Unbroken Circle.

John and Millie Youngberg, directors
Family Life International
Andrews University
Berrien Springs, MI 49104, USA
June 1996

CHAPTER

1

THE OLD HOME PLACE

Family Dynamics

(**Millie**) The United Airlines jet wings its way through the friendly skies, heading south. I'm going home. In the old days, I would arrive at the busy Rosenberg, Texas, train station just a couple of miles from the homeplace and be met by Cousin Millie in the old Model A. But the old-fashioned Rosenberg Depot is no longer the hub of community transportation. It just remains the center of a lot of memories from bygone years.

We've arrived at the Houston Intercontinental Terminal— I follow the baggage signs and pick up my suitcase. Alamo car rental arrows direct me out the doors into balmy Texas breezes. I climb onto the Alamo shuttle and am whisked past two other terminals, through bustling traffic, to the car rental office.

They tell me and everyone else in the long line of customers that because of a recent storm, the computer reservation service is down. I sort through my purse for my travel agent's confirmation slip, with its all-important reservation number. During what seems an endless wait as the agent-in-training fills out the necessary paperwork, I restlessly tap my foot, anxious to be on my way to the destination of the old home place. One step closer.

The roads are under construction. It seems that when one is endeavoring to get home quickly, the road department specifically plans as many detours and obstacles as possible. The highways around the airport are not that familiar to me. While waiting at red lights, I steal glances at the road map to get my bearings. At last I'm heading down more familiar freeways to my little hometown.

My mind recalls all those other times I've returned home: from a hectic, active, involved year at college—or from a challenging year of teaching. It always felt so good to be able to collapse and rest—just to be home again. Arriving was always an exciting moment. Dashing up through the back porch, the chances were I'd find Cousin Millie running to greet me from the kitchen, where she had been preparing some of those delectable Czechoslovakian pastries. We would meet in a wonderfully comforting hug, Cousin Millie and I. She was the mother figure in my life, and I would, of course, proceed to tell her about the trip home. Those trips could be quite eventful. On one, the train I was on sped head-on into another oncoming train. That year, a stranger brought me safely home. How thankful I was for a safe arrival.

After a rushed greeting with Cousin Millie, I would race from one room to another, detecting changes and inspecting new or familiar items of interest. I would deposit my luggage in my bedroom with its floral pink-and-white wallpaper and with its water stains on the ceiling—in the shape of clouds, faces, and bears—caused by one of the last hurricanes. It had always looked like this, from the time I'd been a little girl. The same pictures would be on the walls, and there would be crispy clean sheets on the bed, smelling, as always, of the sun and the Texas air where they were hung out to dry. The starched curtains my mother had been known for would be blowing in the same southern Texas breezes that had perfumed the sheets. It was my room, in my home—and I would be glad to be there.

But today I'm going home, and it is different. Mother and father have been resting in their graves for sixty years, awaiting the resurrection morning. Cousin Millie, who raised my brother George and me, and whom we affectionately called "Milko," closed her eyes in death just six months ago. This time, no one will be there to greet me and welcome me home with open arms. The old home place will be empty.

The house that had been painted fresh white now has patches of mildew, and the paint is peeling off in flakes. When Dad built the house to accommodate his family in the 1930s, it had been a well-constructed, respectable, attractive home. My mother enhanced it with her lovely roses, white lilies, and other fragrant flowers. Dad felt that every home should have fruit and nut trees around it that not only provided shade but also produced food, so there were plum, pear, fig, and pecan trees to grace the place.

When the pecan trees were productive, Cousin Millie had faithfully gathered the pecans from under the trees and would then spend hours laboriously shelling the cracked pecans on winter evenings. It was almost a ritual. And then, at our yearly Christmas visit, Milko would proudly go to the deep freezer and pull out five or ten pounds of fresh pecans and present them to us as her gift of love. We never objected to receiving them.

I remembered how John, my dear husband, and I had spent days painting the exterior of the old place. Poor John ended up with white spray paint over much of his face, giving him a ghostly appearance. But Cousin Millie swelled with pride when the job was accomplished. With obvious glee, Milko told us how a neighbor lady had said that it was the nicest white house in all of Rosenberg. So she decided to call it the White House, just like the residence of the president of the United States. It was her home, and it was George's home, and it was my home.

Now I eagerly open the door to the memories of life as I enter the house. Somehow, it feels strange, as though I'm now intruding. The same creaky screen door at the back still protests when opened onto the porch. Then there is the kitchen where Cousin Millie cooked so many well-balanced, nutritious, and delicious meals with love. When she first came to live with us after my parents died, all she knew how to make was Jell-O, but it wasn't long until her cakes were the most sought-after desserts of the neighborhood kids and friends, and her meals were delectable.

Milko made Friday evenings a special delight, with Czech pastries filled with luscious fruit fillings and sprinkled with white powdered sugar, or cinnamon rolls packed with raisins and pecans from our own trees and oozing with delicious caramel filling. Yes, my home was special, but it wasn't just the food that made it so.

Now I saunter into the kitchenette, where Milko read to me about the children of Israel crossing the desert. I could hardly wait in anticipation of the next Sabbath night, when we would read the subsequent episode in the exciting story. A subtle thread of spirituality ran through the old home place, like an answer to a mother's prayer. It was part of the important transmission of a religious heritage that has affected my whole life. I will treasure it, because it was that infusion of love for God that helped push me forward in my spiritual journey of life, and by God's grace, that journey will end in an eternal home.

I enter the dining room. There is the big, solid, round, dark-oak table. On the wall still hangs the picture of the children walking over the broken bridge on a stormy night, the guardian angel guiding their footsteps. A smile comes to my face as I remember how sure I was, even as a child, of my guardian angel's care.

In my parents' bedroom, I can see myself as a little girl sick on that bed with an extremely high temperature from scarlet fever. Sixty years later, I can still see my mother lying in that same bed in a diabetic coma. Doctors didn't know how to diagnose or treat the illness appropriately back in the '30s. She never awoke from that coma.

Sleeping porches were in style back in those days. The three walls of windows allowed sufficient breeze to let us sleep in the sultry southern Texas summers. It was from this porch that my father had shouted for me to call the doctor. He was having severe chest pains. As a nine-year-old, I was terrified at the responsibility of getting a doctor to save my father's life. The doctor arrived but was helpless. Within minutes, Dad, who had grieved his heart out during the preceding six weeks since my mother's death, was gone.

Now the old sleeping porch is filled with furniture from that bygone era. There is the old upright Philco radio cabinet from which George and I would listen to *The Lone Ranger*. I crawl over fans, steady myself on the old wardrobe closet, and stumble over to the cedar chest. Inside are George's merchant marine uniforms from World War II. Christmas presents—never used—are still in their original boxes on the bed. The clothes hanging in the wardrobe closet were quite fashionable in the 1940s, but by now they have no value and are draped over old-fashioned clothes hangers, moth-eaten and covered with dust and decorated with cobwebs. The sleeping porch has become a family museum.

As I walk into the living room, two sets of eyes look at me with warmth and gentle smiles—my parents' old wedding photo. They've been gone so long that memories of them are faint, but they were my life's roots and provided me with the home that has been my foundation. And here is the old stuffed chair, where I struggled through homework or relaxed and read a favorite storybook, with my legs dangling over the sturdy upholstered arms. This is where school friends would gather to thoroughly discuss the day or make plans for another.

And then there's the attic. The rope that made it easier to climb the steep stairs is still there, so I pull myself up. It is hot and stuffy. Here at the top of the stairs is my little doll bed, surrounded with cobwebs. There is the toy chest of drawers and kitchen cabinet that I played with for endless hours as a child, as I spun dreams that someday I would have my own home and cook food and be important like my mother and father. Now they are cobweb-covered, waiting for another child to play with them.

The old home place had a special air of enchantment about it. When I went out into the cold world of school, I sometimes didn't perform as others expected me to. Sometimes on the playground there would be angry voices if I didn't hit the ball right or spell a word correctly in the spelling bee. But in my childhood heart of wonder, if I could get home, everything would be all right.

As I visit my memories again, I long to go back to those times and to the old home place. John and I now have our own home and a cabin in the Blue Ridge Mountains. I'm hopeful that these places will be as cherished in our children's and grandchildren's memories as is the mystical Texas home for me.

John's oldest brother, Stephen, missed his childhood home in South Dakota so much that at age sixteen he ran away from home in the Lower Rio Grande Valley to go back and relive the wondrous times of before. He was riding in a boxcar, heading for South Dakota, when he met a couple of homeless bums.

"Boy," one of them asked, "where are you headed? You say you're running away from home? Do you have a dad and mom who love you?"

"Yeah," Stephen answered, "they love me."

"Then what are you doing out here with us bums?" The bum swore at him and said, "Get out of here and go HOME!"

Since time began, our ancestors—remote and more recent—have all had the same inexpressible desire to go "back home." This goes all the way back to Adam and Eve as they slowly turned their backs on the lovely home with vines, trees, and flowers they had fashioned with their own hands. As they passed through the gates of Eden, the unquenchable desire to someday go back home welled up in their hearts. I think the nostalgia for the old home place that I have felt ever since I left home at age nineteen, is something God has hidden in the heart of every soul. I believe it is almost innate to long to return to the garden. We all dream of going back home. In reality, we can never go back in time and fully recapture the moments of charm and innocence. The old home place will suffer from termites, the roof will sag, and the ceiling will have watermarks resembling fantasy animals and maps of faraway places. If time should last, our present home place will also decay and ultimately disintegrate.

But the real home we are all longing for in our heart-of-hearts is the palace God and His angels are preparing for us in a better land.

CHAPTER

2

THE FIRST HOME

(Millie) It was finished! All the careful plans and dreams had now been transformed into a beautiful garden home. Even God was pleased, saying, "Now, THIS is very good!" The onlooking angels had been lost in the beauty of the Creator's handiwork. They had gazed eagerly and with great interest and curiosity as the master design unfolded quickly, one surprise following another. Truly, Eden was magnificent. It had happened like this:

The angels watch enthusiastically from their vantage point as the Spirit of God hovers over empty darkness and water. Suddenly, a strange light begins shining. As the total blackness separates into light and darkness, the angels learn of a creative concept for a new world: day. Day one, to be exact.

A deafening roar follows God's command as water separates from water and a vast, empty sky expands above a dry, barren land. The gathered water forms into an enormous sea. Dark and light, land, water, empty sky. It is all eerily empty and accompanied by an almost chilling silence. Day two. Darkness slides over it all—and angels sing of the mighty power that made the mountains rise.

The First Home

Day three: Small and delicate, fresh green spring grasses appear. The green carpet raises its delicate blades and covers the land. Lofty trees stretch heavenward, each with its own kind of leaves and delicious fruits and nuts in a variety of shapes and colors. Gardens of nutritious and colorful vegetables form, with not a weed in sight. The fragrance of the flowers that grace the landscape perfumes the air. Pink and lavender orchids, tiny blue forget-me-nots, thornless roses in all shades, white lilies that stretch upward, and thousands of other creative beauties adorn the landscape. And once again, God is pleased, saying, "It is good!"

The scientific balance is added next—sunshine—the fourth day. The sun shines brightly, bathing the earth with just the perfect amount of warmth and bringing the light the plants need to live. The immense, pulsing, fiery ball of the sun begins to dance with the earth in rotations just right for seasons and days and nights. And then there is twilight: Stars come into view, some exploding into their God-given positions. Then, silently and gracefully, a large silver ball appears, shedding its delicate, pale beams over all God's creative gifts of love. The angels stand in awe as they silently look at the Creator's work, then in evening worship burst forth in a glorious harmony of praise at the day's new creations. All is so perfect, so synchronized, so scientific—so mysterious.

"What is there to do next?" the angels inquire. On the fifth day, the Creator again speaks. The waters are to have living creatures, and the sky is to have birds that fly and sing within the great green forest cathedrals. There will be myriads of combinations and configurations, shapes and contours, hues and shades of colors. Some will be known as male and some will be female. By twilight, the increasingly exquisite and beautiful garden is burgeoning with life. The day's work is completed; birds join the angels in eventide worship by warbling and chirping songs of praise, accompanied by the hum of swaying trees in the breeze. Again, it is good.

There are to be other creatures—and these are to dwell on the land. Some will graze in the meadows, some will be little creatures that dart about on the ground, and there will even be wild beasts to roam the wooded areas. The Creator makes them male and female on this busy sixth day, and in thousands of unique forms, they spread over the earth. The angels observe that these creatures of the land seem to find their own kind and pair off by twos. Something still seems to be missing in the perfection. What will be the added element?

A council has been held: the Father with the Son and the Spirit. It is announced that the Three will "make man in our image, in our likeness" (Gen. 1:26, NIV). They have decided just how to create the new creature, with all functional parts working together in a state of wholeness and well-being, of purpose and action: He is to rule over the fish in the sea, the birds that fly and the wildlife that moves on the ground. And the plants and fruits are his food (Gen. 1:28, 29).

The Creator and the created—in one image. And here the Creator pauses, waiting for the newly created being to sense the need for the crowning act of Creation. To do this, God gives him a task: naming the animals. The man sees that there is a male and female lion, a male and female giraffe, a male and female dolphin. He realizes that he is all alone in the garden. He is lonesome, and now he discovers with joy that God's intention for all creation is that they dwell in relation to others as well as to God. God says, "It is not good. It is not good for man to be alone." Someone is missing. Quickly, the creative plan continues.

Woman: radiant with life, intelligence, loveliness—a richly compatible companion to man. Together they have dominion over their garden home called Eden. It is made beautiful, complete, and without decay. All they need to make them happy is here. Food to eat, beauty to look upon, never-ending learning—all exist for their enjoyment.

The First Home

It is the first wedding service. Angels and birds are ready for the wedding march. The fragrance of the garden, the living green and petals of color create an atmosphere just right for this once-in-a-lifetime service of commitment. God brings Eve to Adam, and with an extra heartbeat, Adam sees how he can be complete with one like himself. God is the source of bringing completeness to them both. God stands with Eve and Adam. Placing her hand in his, God blesses them. "Leave, cleave, and have one flesh," He says. As the sun sets and the created Sabbath day of rest is about to begin, God moves away, and Adam and Eve begin their journey of life together in their perfect home. In the silence is heard the gentle voice of God, like an echo of their own thoughts, "Behold, it is *very* good." It is the first life, the first marriage, the first Sabbath, the first beginnings of a freshly created earth—and it is all very good!

Adam and Eve were perfectly suited to each other. It was part of God's plan to give them everything that would bring joy and happiness in their new home. Their surroundings were exceedingly beautiful: delicious fruits, graceful shrubs, colorful plants, flowers, birds, fish and animals, delicate fragrances, and the high-fidelity songs of fluttering birds filling the air. Everything in the garden home spoke of God's great love for Adam and Eve. It was for their pleasure, and they delighted in it. There were no problems, no tears, no pain. It was just plain heavenly. Pleasurable labor also brought happiness and companionship as they joined together in the work God had given them to do in their home environment.

The garden home was also a school where daily exhilarating instruction from the Creator electrified their beings. They were to teach their children in the home, using nature as the curriculum designed by the Creator. Luxuriant vines, swaying trees loaded with delicious fruits and nuts or graceful verdant leaves, birds singing their own praise to the Father, and small creeping things that had their part in the balance of nature, were all part of the lesson book.

In the center of their garden home were two trees. One was the Tree of Life. Continuing to eat of its luscious fruit would enable them to live forever. The other was the Tree of Knowledge of Good and Evil. Far beyond any imaginable beauty, it was like shining gold, with silver fruit glimmering in the sun. It, too, was part of their lesson book for life. It taught the importance of trusting God's Word as supreme, overriding the feelings and the senses. It was important they understood that the key to happiness is found in living out God's Word by obeying His one simple command: You shall *not* eat the fruit on this tree (Gen. 2:17).

They had a happy and contented life and a home established for the benefit of all future generations.

Worship in the Eden home

After a delightful day eating luscious fruit and training vines into arbors for their new home, Adam and Eve watched the sun descend in the west. Heaven and earth seemed ready to touch as the rich colors of gold, orange, pink, and purple flowed across the sky. It was then that the first pair heard the voice of God calling them in the cool of the day. They answered their Creator Friend, invited Him into their new home, and with joy showed Him the arbors of thornless roses, bougainvillea, and delicate vines their hands had been weaving into living walls and a roof. They raised their voices in songs of praise and gratitude, adoring and bowing before their Creator and God as He talked with them. The birds in the lofty heights picked up the strains, and angels all around them answered in a ten-part refrain. The hearts of Adam and Eve swelled with joy and gratefulness, their unimpaired six or seven—or possibly ten—senses registering the beauty of it all in their memories. Jesus assured them of His unfailing love, and as He returned heavenward, He called out, "Lo, I am with you always." A perfect stillness and peace descended on the garden. A gentle lion purred nearby. The animals, each in their own language, praised their Maker as they prepared for the night's repose. A perfect day had ended.

That was *worship* in a perfect home. Worship is accepting and expressing, in gratitude to God, that you are realizing and rejoicing in a gift in which you had no part. And just think, God had planned that an eternity of even happier days should follow for Adam and Eve, their children, their great-great-great-grand-children—all the way down to us—as we all learned to know God.

The cooing of mourning doves woke Adam and Eve the following morning in their freshly built home, the sun peeping over the rolling hills. Their first thoughts were of praise to God. In rapturous joy, they sang glory to their Friend. Overflowing love for beauty beyond imagination filled their hearts with praise to their Creator. A passing cheetah paused to listen as heaven and earth blended their voices in praise. Other worlds looked on with delight at this worshipful moment in the Eden home. A harmonious melody sweetened the atmosphere of their perfect garden—a garden now slightly damp with the morning dew. Nature, with the fragrance of its delicate flowers, blended its note of joy into the incense of praise and worship. The perfect landscape foliage spoke of God's great love and law. What heights of ecstasy were experienced when Adam and Eve "converse[d] with leaf and flower and tree, gathering from each the secrets of its life" (*Patriarchs and Prophets*, p. 51).

Can you add to this already majestic scene by imagining God Himself being there in their home, quietly instructing them and sharing in their excitement of discovering the marvels of the universe? He planned to continue teaching and sharing with them throughout the ages. They would eat from the Tree of Life and live forever and ever. The angels looked at it all taking place, and as they watched in awe, they burst into praise, adding to the beauty of the Garden.

The angels' praise reached a new crescendo—"Behold, it is very good!"

During those early hours of worship in the garden, Adam and Eve learned the mysteries of creation from the lips of the Creator. Each discovery was an insight into the character of God —an insight into balance, the love of beauty, variety, pleasure, a sense of humor, and the desire for His creatures to be happy. Love and gratitude overflowed into praise and worship. Daily, they became more in tune with the divine music of love that filled an unfallen world.

That was life in the first home a long time ago. Their Creator wanted Adam and Eve to be happy forever after, and they would—as long as they lived one simple principle—God's Word is to be supreme in the life.

For your family

1. Using the Bible and the writings of Ellen White such as *Patriarchs and Prophets*, awaken your *sanctified imagination* and write your own Garden of Eden story to share during family worship. The authors will be happy to receive the creative works of children and teens up to sixteen years of age. For the most outstanding and usable creative work, a $50 award will be given each year until 1999 (unless Jesus comes before then) if conditions make this possible. (It is understood that the authors of this book have the right to publish any submission, giving appropriate credit.) Send to John and Millie Youngberg, Marriage and Family Commitment, Andrews University, Berrien Springs, MI 49104.

2. Dad and Mom, share at worship time what home was like when you were growing up and the spiritual journey that began there.

3. What is special about your home now?

CHAPTER

3

HE MADE IT!

Seven generations from Adam (but while Adam was still alive), a babe was born. A tide of corruption seemed to be engulfing the planet when the first person identified in Scripture as a prophet appeared. His name was Enoch. We don't know much about him. Genesis dedicates six verses to him; Hebrews, one verse; and Jude, two verses. That's it! But these nine verses are hard-hitting, sublime, and full of hope.

First of all, what did he prophesy about? Jude 14 and 15 tell us that he prophesied about the second coming of Christ and the great judgment day. His was not a popular message in a day when people were more interested in feeling good and doing their own thing. Yet Enoch spoke of a hope that Jesus would come and take us away from our earthly sojourn to the heavenly home.

Enoch as a father

Tucked in among the genealogies is the message that Enoch had a son at age sixty-five. Parenting brought a new dimension to his own interpersonal relationships. Even more important, as he sensed his love for his son and his son's love for him, he progressed to a whole new stage in his own spiritual development. In our marriage seminars, we often have said marriage is a school that teaches us love and skills we probably wouldn't learn any other way. It is a school of discipline, of trial, and of sacrifice that polishes and refines us. And when children come—wow! That is truly "higher" education!

"Enoch walked with God *after he begat Methuselah* three hundred years, and begat sons and daughters" (Gen. 5:22, KJV, emphasis supplied).

Enoch took fathering seriously. He gave his little son a rather unique name. Literally, it meant "when he dies, it will come." Methuselah's very name was a living prophecy of the 969 years of his life—that when he died, the Flood would come. Almost a thousand years went by while Methuselah stood for the same principles his father, Enoch, had lived by before him. In the year that he died, the world was destroyed by the Flood.

Enoch walked with God

In his book *Finding God*, family counselor Larry Crabb brings out some fascinating insights based on the life of Enoch. In Genesis 5, the genealogies list ten men, starting with Adam, moving on down through Seth, and ending with Noah. All these men are said to have "lived" after they became fathers, except Noah, whose story continues in later chapters, and Enoch. While the other men merely *lived*, Enoch *walked with God*. What is the difference between "living out" your allotted years and "walking with God"? Walking with God connotes my following God in His paths and not merely asking Him to bless me in mine. Amos 3:3 asks, "Can two walk together, except they be agreed?" (KJV).

Enoch was the seventh generation from Adam, through Seth. However, the seventh from Adam through Cain was Lamech. Lamech stood for a whole different perspective on life. He was the first recorded polygamist of history, and he bragged to his two wives of how he was even willing to kill someone if it meant getting his own way. He said, "Wives of Lamech, hear my words. I have killed a man for wounding me, a young man for injuring me" (Gen. 4:23, NIV). Lamech typifies the many people who are more interested in the healing of their hurts, by whatever means, than they are in walking with God, whatever the trials and problems. Hebrews 11:6 establishes the basic principle that our one priority in life should be pleasing God—whatever that takes and whatever it costs—and that we do this by coming to God on His terms and believing that a heavenly home exists as a reward for all those who diligently seek Him. The Bible hall-of-fame illustration that the author of Hebrews gives to prove the point is Enoch:

> By faith Enoch was taken away so that he did not see death, and was not found, because God had taken him; for before he was taken he had this testimony, that he pleased God (Hebrews 11:6).

The bottom line is this: "I must surrender my fascination with myself for a more worthy preoccupation with the character and purposes of God. I am not the point. He is. I exist for Him. He does not exist for me" (*Finding God*, 41). Enoch learned this lesson more than any other antediluvian. He represents families in the last days of earth's history who will be translated to heaven without seeing death—who are more interested in God's glory than in soothing their own hurts and understanding their own egos. Is it possible? Could our family ever make it back to the Eden home? Good news! Going home? A relative already made it!

A little girl was asked how Enoch walked with God. "It was this way," she said. "Enoch and God were good friends. They used to go on walks together. Each day they would walk a little farther than the day before. The walks got longer and longer. One day they were walking along and were having such a good time talking that they went farther and farther.

Suddenly Enoch realized that it was getting late and said that he must hurry back home if he was to get there before dark. But God said, 'Enoch, we've walked so far that it's closer to my home than it is to yours. Come on home with Me!' "

"And Enoch walked with God: and he was not; for God took him" (Gen. 5:24, KJV).

For your family

1. How did Enoch walk with God?

For children: Tell the simple story of Enoch walking with God. Have the children draw pictures of Enoch walking with God to heaven.

For adults and youth: What do you think walking with God has to do with work, daily duties, daily interaction with friends, or with commercial dealings? With meditation, mystical experiences, or altered states of consciousness?

2. What secrets can you find in the following Ellen White quote for walking with God?

> "In the midst of a life of active labor, Enoch stead-fastly maintained his communion with God. The greater and more pressing his labors, the more constant and earnest were his prayers. He continued to exclude himself, at certain periods, from all society. After remaining for a time among the people, laboring to benefit them by instruction and example, he would withdraw, to spend a season in solitude, hungering and thirsting for that divine knowledge which God alone can impart. Communing thus with God, Enoch came more and more to reflect the divine image. His face was radiant with a holy light, even the light that shineth in the face of Jesus. As he came forth from these divine communings, even the ungodly beheld with awe the impress of heaven upon his countenance. . . .

He Made It!

"The greater the existing iniquity, the more earnest was his longing for the home of God. While still on earth, he dwelt, by faith, in the realms of light. . . .

"For three centuries he had walked with God. Day by day he had longed for a closer union; nearer and nearer had grown the communion, until God took him to himself. He had stood at the threshold of the eternal world, only a step between him and the land of the blest; and now the portals opened, the walk with God, so long pursued on earth, continued, and he passed through the gates of the Holy City—the first from among men to enter there" (*Patriarchs and Prophets*, 86, 87).

3. Have marriage and parenthood been schools of discipline for you? Do you have any friends who have chosen to drop out of the school of marriage or the school of parenthood? How do you feel about this?

4. Has having to live with your spouse, your brothers and sisters, or your parents been a school in helping to polish your character? What positive changes have occurred as a result of marriage and parenting?

5. How could your family "walk with God"? List seven specific ways. What plans could you make to implement these?

6. Some skeptics claim there are no eternal rewards. According to them, this earth, with its joys and its sorrows, is all there is. How do you think the life of Enoch and his translation—"both of the righteous and the wicked . . . had witnessed his departure" *(Patriarchs and Prophets*, 88)—might have affected the skeptics of his time? How might the fact that somebody made it back to "The First Home" have affected the righteous?

4

THE ARK'S READY!

Is the Family Ready?

By faith Noah, being divinely warned of things not yet seen, moved with godly fear, prepared an ark for the saving of his household, by which he condemned the world and became heir of the righteousness which is according to faith (Hebrews 11:7, NKJV).

Can a God-fearing family survive the corruption of these last days? Is it possible to raise children for the Lord in an age of prevailing iniquity?

A few decades after Adam's death, Noah was born. He, like Enoch before him, is distinguished in the genealogy not just for *living* but for *walking* with God (Gen. 6:9). Noah did this in an age when "God saw that the wickedness of man was great in the earth, and that every imagination of the thoughts of his heart was only evil continually" (Gen. 6:5, KJV). Somehow, Noah stood apart from the rest.

What were the sins that characterized the world just before the Flood? Ellen White writes that the people were violent, basely corrupt, hardened, and had given themselves over entirely to the indulgence of appetite. Their passions knew no control. The people trusted the imaginations of their

The Ark's Ready!

own hearts and didn't care to know the will of God. Christ pointed to their unbelief as an illustration of how things will be in the days when He will come the second time. "But as the days of Noe were, so shall also the coming of the Son of man be. For as in the days that were before the flood they were eating and drinking, marrying and giving in marriage, until the day that Noe entered into the ark, and knew not until the flood came, and took them all away; so shall also the coming of the Son of man be" (Matt. 24:37-39, KJV).

Eating is not wrong in and of itself. But eating to excess and gluttony is. Drinking is not wrong if we drink the right things. Yet apparently the cravings of the antediluvians knew no control. Marriage and sexuality are blessings, but Noah's contemporaries interpreted privilege as license. In brief, the generation before the Flood considered the *summum bonum* of life to be eating, drinking, and indulging itself. That which God had given as gifts showing His tender care, they abused and debased.

All this happened in a time of apparent prosperity—prosperity that crept into a position of supreme importance. As God was replaced by the passion for riches and luxury, people not only forgot the importance of their Creator but also the dignity and rights of others. Property and marriage companionship were no longer secure. If someone wanted another's wife, he took her by force. If someone wanted another's property, he seized it violently.

God looked down, appalled and heartbroken, at the degeneracy of a people created but a millennium and a half earlier. The imagination of their hearts was only evil continually. Only divine intervention and a new start could save the world. He looked down and saw one family—a husband, a wife, and three children—who loved Him enough to live His way. Through this family, He would give one last message of repentance and hope to a lost world.

An angel came to the husband, Noah, and announced

God's plan to destroy the earth by water in 120 years. Along with this horrifying announcement came a directive to prepare a huge boat for the salvation of those who repented and for the animal species God had originally created. The Divine Architect gave specific plans for this "ark." Noah invested all he had in building it. Progress was slow because of the hardness of the wood and the necessary carefulness of every joint. To build a boat 450 feet long with three decks was no small project. Gradually, the hull and superstructure took shape.

Immense crowds came to see the spectacle of a man building the largest boat ever known up to that time—and building it on dry land. Although every hammer blow and cut of the saw was an eloquent sermon that Noah believed the Flood was coming, he would pause at regular intervals during each day and address the crowds of people, urging them to repent of their selfish living and to return to the Lord. At first a number believed, but as the years lengthened into decades and then into a century, scoffing and ridicule took the place of belief. Some of the carpenters who worked on the ark accepted Noah's message. Some of these backslid with the passing of the years; others died before the Flood. Noah's grandfather, Methuselah, his sons, and their sons believed and helped in the building of the ark. Methuselah, whose name meant "when he dies, it will come," died the very year of the Flood at the advanced age of 969.

After 120 years of arduous work, the hammers fell silent. Pitch was applied both inside and out to seal any hidden cracks between the massive timbers. You know the story, but it is still hard to grapple with the reality—long lines of animals that came out of the woods two by two. In perfect order, they went into the huge ark. Pairs of all kinds of birds dived and danced into the dark hull as well. People were momentarily impressed with the singular occurrences and probably consulted with the sages, philosophers, and renowned scientists of the time. The experts probably had the answers: the events were rare phenomena that happened from time to time—they presaged no crisis. A flood was a scientific impossibility. God Himself, if there was a God, was subject to invariable laws that precluded any catastrophic deluge. Noah? He was insane.

> The time comes when the last appeal of Noah is made to the guilty race. He bids them yet once again heed the message of warning and find refuge in the ark. He stretches out his hands in supplication with voice full of sympathy. With quivering lip and tearful eye, he tells them his work is done, but the loud, coarse mocking and scoffs and insults more determined are heaped upon Noah. Enthusiast, fanatic, crazy, falls upon his ear. He bids them all farewell, he and his family enter the ark (Ellen White, *This Day With God*, 235).

A blinding flash illuminated the landscape. An angel descended from heaven and slowly closed the mighty door. It was massive. Noah and his sons could neither close it nor open it. The thud of its closing left Noah's family locked inside, unable to leave. For seven days, Noah and his family waited within the ark. Still, no flood came. The time of delay must have been a severe trial to Noah; however, the time was occupied busily in adjusting cargo, settling animals in, and making ready for the storm. The sight of the angel and the remembrance of the pairs of animals—some of them by nature ferocious and some of them domestic—entering the ark peacefully and in perfect order as if guided by unseen hands left many around the ark feeling uneasy. They were fearful of impending doom and wishing they were inside the ark. However, with the passing of days, their disbelief and revelry soon returned. The apparent delay confirmed to those on the outside that Noah's message was a delusion. "Notwithstanding the solemn scenes which they had witnessed . . . they still continued their sport and revelry, even making a jest of these signal manifestations of God's power. They gathered in crowds about the ark, deriding its inmates with a daring violence which they had never ventured upon before" (*Conflict and Courage*, 40).

That closed door parallels the close of probation at the end of the world. There will come a moment when the last sermon is preached, the last call is made, the last message-filled book is given to a neighbor. Fathers, mothers, and children will receive the last gracious invitation to accept God's plan for their lives and yield Him implicit obedience. Loyalty to God and obedience to His commandments above the commandments of men will be the test. Some will be outside God's offer of safety; some will be inside.

> Come, my people, enter your chambers, and shut your doors behind you; Hide yourself, as it were, for a little moment, until the indignation is past. For behold, the Lord comes out of His place to punish the inhabitants of the earth for their iniquity; The earth will also disclose her blood, and will no more cover her slain (Isa. 26:20, 21).

After seven days, someone pointed to the horizon where ominous dark clouds formed. Presently, the whole sky displayed an eerie blackness. Then, rain—lightly at first. People continued to hurl their insults and jests at Noah. The rain came in torrents. Lightning flashed from the sky, destroying stately palaces and idolatrous shrines, scattering their ruins across the landscape. As the fury of the storm increased, wild animals came running to human beings as if asking their help. Some parents tied their children to the backs of beasts, knowing that these would seek higher ground. There were no more jokes. Frantically, people beat their fists on the side of the ark, begging for admittance: "Let us in!" They pleaded to Noah and God to save them, but the only answer was the shrieking of the gale, mixed with the echo of their own baleful cries above the confusion of the storm. The fountains of the deep were unstopped. Thunder from above met thunder from below, as water spewed from the ground with unbelievable force, throwing huge boulders hundreds of feet into the air. Water poured from the skies in torrents. Forgotten were the unanswerable arguments and explanations of the great philosophers. There would be no more arguments, explanations, or chances. It was too late. The door was closed!

Perhaps some would say that Noah wasn't a very successful evangelist. He preached 120 years, and in the end how many converts did he have? Second Peter 2:5 says that only eight were saved: Noah himself, his wife, his three children—Shem, Ham, and Japheth—and his three daughters-in-law. Noah's preaching didn't save the world, but he did save all his own family.

> By faith Noah, being divinely warned of things not yet seen, moved with godly fear, prepared an ark for the saving of his household, by which he condemned the world and became heir of the righteousness which is according to faith (Hebrews 11:7).

Christ said, "As the days of Noe were, so shall also the coming of the Son of man be" (Matt. 24:37, KJV). What hope is there for our children? With fathers and mothers who "walk with God" and with children who follow the modeling of their parents, what will we have? Whole families saved for the kingdom! Is your home an ark—an ark of safety where the Word of God is of supreme and highest priority? Can it be said of you, as it was of the patriarch of old, "Noah found grace in the eyes of the Lord. . . . Noah was a just man, perfect in his generations. Noah walked with God. . . . Thus Noah did; according to all that God commanded him, so he did?" (Genesis 6:8, 9, 22).

Will you follow God, even in the face of peers and a whole generation who scoff and ridicule? As probation's door closes, there will be such families. They have knelt together in family worship. They have claimed Jesus' blood daily in their lives. Already, they are preparing spiritually. While the world will be outside, they will be secure in God's ark—families of the heavenly King to proclaim His glory for eternal ages.

For your family

1. How do you think Noah's children felt when the ark was finished, the animals came in, the door was closed, and there was no rain for seven days?

2. Is there anything in your life preventing you from entering into God's ark of safety? What is it?

3. When we say No to God, it is like going on a sled down a big hill. At first one could change his or her mind and stop the sled. But the faster it goes, the harder it is to get off. What do you think are the most important sins taking the world downhill today? Which of those sins are affecting the church the most?

4. It took 120 years of careful, arduous work to prepare an ark that would save Noah's family. What long-term actions/plans/preparations do you see God calling you to make to strengthen your family in preparation for Christ's coming?

5. Have children draw an ark on a big piece of paper. Using old magazines, cut out pictures of animals and paste them on the paper. Have the children give this "work of art" a name. Suggest they put a snapshot of themselves and the family into the picture and post the finished work in your family exhibition gallery.

CHAPTER
5

A WOMAN'S DRAMA

"Noah, my dear, you look tired this evening. How was the day? You say your back hurts from carrying those heavy timbers? Here—let me rub some liniment into your aching muscles. You know, dear, today I was figuring that so far I've prepared 9,300 dinners for you and the crew that are working on the ark. And when you count the afternoon snack, that makes 18,600 food preparations for the crew. You know, Noah, I'm just about running out of recipes. There are only so many ways that I can cook gluten. You know—beans and gluten, gluten and beans . . .

"Noah, I'm concerned about Ham. Since they built the grandstands and the rock bands have been giving concerts for the tour groups coming through, well, I hope he's not being influenced. You'll be happy to know, dear, that the girls and I finished loading Storage Room C in the ark with two tons of dried apricots this afternoon. I also got those 200-kilo bags of dried prunes and the bags of almonds into Storage Room B.

"Noah, that Ladies Aid Society came by again this morning. They had the columnist of the *Mesopotamian Tablet* with them. Some of them asked questions just dripping with sarcasm. I was praying that God would give me the right words to speak. One of them lingered behind afterward and told me that in her heart she believed the message you and I have stood for all these years and that if she could only convince her husband, she might join us in the ark. Noah, it was so encouraging to hear her say that. I've been feeling all the ridicule and antagonism lately—it's been overwhelming.

"Some of the students from the U of M were especially bad today, weren't they? Let me wash off your shirt where they splattered you with rotten eggs. May God forgive them. I saw the one young man blowing marijuana smoke in your face, asking if your trip would be better than his. Noah, even though everyone else rejects us, I want you to know I am so happy we have each other and our three boys, and that they married lovely, godly girls. And Noah, I'm thankful that you're doing exactly what the angel told you to do. It's been hard and long, but I know we are on God's side in this great controversy. God has chosen us to do something special for Him."

We know almost nothing about her, only that she married Noah, had three sons, and was part of the family that began the earth again. We don't even know her name.

Her very obscurity may be helpful to us though. What would it have been like to be that woman, Mrs. Noah? To experience her feelings, her trials, her faith? As a woman— a very human one?

For your family

Form a family or a group reading circle. Read Genesis 6 and 7 together, perhaps taking turns. Take more than one evening if your time together is limited. Follow up the reading of Genesis 6 and 7 with a discussion that starts with the following:

1. If you woke up one morning to have your husband tell you that he had dreamed a dream in which an angel told

him to take all your life's savings and build a boat 450 feet long and three decks high, what would you say?

2. Would you feel the same way about it forty years later? Seventy years later?

3. Do you think Noah's wife had the same set of values as he did? Why?

4. The book *Patriarchs and Prophets* talks about the sins of the antediluvians and uses terms such as *excess*, *extravagance*, *luxury*, and *display*. In our day, what would you consider to be *excess*? Enough? Not enough? Do you think Noah's wife had enough?

5. How do you think Noah's wife survived as a parent?

Keeping the home fires burning

Carrying heavy responsibilities in educating three lively sons

Praying for the salvation of her children

Facing the "teen years"—which may have lasted fifty years back in those days!

6. Do you think Noah's wife had any other women to encourage her in the Women's Ministry Seminar she held with her three daughters-in-law? How do you think she handled her stresses?

7. What kind of feelings do you think Noah's wife had as a woman, a mother, and as a neighbor after the work on the ark had been going on for a hundred years?

8. What character traits do you think Noah's wife had? Why? Did she take time for her own spiritual growth when there was so much work to do? How did she maintain self-acceptance? A good self-concept?

9. What is the story of Noah's wife saying to *us* as a family? What is the story saying to you?

10. Under the following five character headings, come up with words, phrases, or concepts from the Bible that indicate that Noah, his wife, and the family possessed these character traits. We suggest you come up with your own. To

get you going, we have some items listed that can be used when your ideas have run out.

Deep religious experience
  1. By faith
  2. My Spirit
  3.

Action-oriented
  4. Moved with fear
  5. Obeyed God—He spoke, they acted
  6.

Simple lifestyle
  7. Invested all they had in the ark
  8.

Had priorities
  9. God came first
 10. Family was very important
 11.

Togetherness
Now, as well as back then, sometimes fathers get most of the credit for big jobs that get done. What words or phrases might indicate attitudes or actions of Noah's wife and the children that were essential to the success of building the ark and saving the family?
 12. Believing in Noah and each other
 13. Supporting and encouraging
 14.

CHAPTER

6

SEEKING A HOMELAND

"They seek a homeland. And truly if they had called to mind that country from which they had come out, they would have had opportunity to return. But now they desire a better, that is, a heavenly country. Therefore God is not ashamed to be called their God, for He has prepared a city for them" (Hebrews 11:14-16, NKJV).

(John) Ever since their banishment from the garden, human beings have sought a home. The vast majority have claimed this earth as their ultimate home. A chosen few have looked beyond, and although they have had to live *in* this world, they have not been *of* this world. They have claimed citizenship in a better country—a heavenly homeland.

According to the chronology of Genesis 5 and 11, Adam's life overlapped that of Methuselah, and Methuselah's life overlapped Shem's. Shem lived six hundred years after the Flood, and because of this, he could have known Abraham. Probably Abraham heard from Shem's lips the account of how God had spared Noah's family in the great deluge. Abraham now became the inheritor of the sacred trust handed down in an unbroken line. Enoch, Methuselah, and Noah had all been pilgrims and strangers on this earth. They were in the world, but not of the world. But with Abraham, being "called out" took on new and added dimensions.

The home Abraham left

Ur of the Chaldees, in 2000 B.C., was a highly civilized city strategically located near where the Tigris-Euphrates Rivers emptied into the Persian Gulf. Archaeologists have removed the desert sands and found abundant evidence of a thriving culture. They have uncovered a school such as Abraham probably attended—where he could have studied reading, writing, arithmetic, and geography. Clay tablets the children used for their learning exercises have been found. Those who picture Abraham as an ignorant nomad are themselves ignorant of the evidence that he was raised in an intellectually stimulating environment and enjoyed the amenities of refinement and comfort. Houses were strongly constructed and usually two stories high. The rooms on the ground floor surrounded a central courtyard, and a stairway led to the second story. The city boasted an efficient sewage system, better, in fact, than many cities in the Middle East today. If it was comfort and a good lifestyle Abraham sought, he need have sought no further. He already had it!

However, in the midst of the flourishing arts and advanced technology, there lurked danger. Idolatry was rampant. Ur's worship places and temple tower have been excavated, all dedicated to pagan deities. The royal tombs show that at a ruler's death, many of his helpers were sacrificed so that they might attend him in the afterlife. Abraham's father, Terah, worshiped idols (see Joshua 24:2).

God's plans to redeem humanity could not find fertile root in Ur. There was need of a fresh start, a break with the past, a "calling out." So the God of glory appeared to Abraham and said to him, "Get out of your country and from your relatives, and come to a land that I will show you" (Acts 7:3). Terah was old; out of respect for him, Abraham took steps to answer God's call as his father's age and health permitted. In stage one, he left Ur and his ancestral tribe. Not being able to cross the Arabian desert with his flocks, he took the longer northern route and journeyed up the Euphrates River together with Terah, his brother Nahor, and his nephew Lot. Because of his father's feebleness, they stopped halfway to Canaan in the rich grasslands of the Euphrates Valley. They named the place Haran in memory of Lot's deceased father and stayed there until Terah died. The country was fertile—the climate ideal. Was this the place to stay?

Second call

After Terah's death, God appeared again to Abraham, renewing the call. Abraham was to leave his relatives and the goodly land of Haran and move forward into Canaan. As a child, I can clearly recall my father preaching on the call of Abraham. He recounted how at age seventy-five Abraham departed from Haran, from the green pastures of the Euphrates:

> So Abram departed as the Lord had spoken to him. Then he took Sarah his wife, and Lot his brother's son, and all their possessions that they had gathered, and the people whom they had acquired in Haran, and they departed to go to the land of Canaan. And into the land of Canaan they came (Gen. 12:4, 5).

My father emphasized the last two phrases—"*They departed to go to the land of Canaan. And into the land of Canaan they came.*" A divine call. A decision to answer the call.

Terah couldn't go on into Canaan. Like Moses a half millennium later, he could see it by the eye of faith, but would not enter, dying on the way to the Promised Land. Nahor, however, could have gone but elected not to. He was probably a sharp businessman like his son Laban after him. Why risk the uncertainties of another land when Haran was so desirable? But Abraham answered the call, whether his brother should choose to join him or not. Life is a journey toward a better hope. God had said "leave"—and leave he did. With his father's death, he was now the head of the encampment. It was forward, ever forward, as God led the way. They crossed the Euphrates, traversed the narrow desert of northern Syria, and then followed the Orontes Valley southward into Canaan. "And into the land of Canaan they came."

Abraham's top priority—knowing God and transmitting this knowledge to His children

A daily custom of Abraham demonstrated that while he lived here on earth, in reality he considered himself a citizen of the heavenly land. This daily (probably morning and evening practice) was that of slaying a lamb and worshiping at an altar. Genesis singles out Abraham as its most prominent altar builder. When Abraham arrived in Canaan at Shechem, "there builded he an altar unto the Lord, who appeared unto him" (Gen. 12:7, KJV). When Abraham moved to Bethel—where years later his grandson Jacob would see the dream of the heavenly ladder—the Bible says, "There he builded an altar unto the Lord, and called upon the name of the Lord" (verse 8, KJV). After Abraham had lied and misrepresented God in Egypt and become disappointed at his own lack of faith, he went back to Bethel, the site where God had appeared to him before. Penitent hands rebuilt the old altar, "and there Abram called on the name of the Lord" (Gen. 13:4, KJV). God appeared to him at the worship altar.

Ellen Harmon, a girl of seventeen, had her first vision

while kneeling at the family altar. Why celebrate morning and evening worship? I believe it is that God will become real to us—so we may know Jesus and claim the merits of His sacrifice over our lives and our children. It is to say to the onlooking universe that there is no priority as high with us as knowing God.

After Abraham's home was blessed with children, a top priority of his was to transmit to their hearts the same desire for a better country that burned in his. God Himself attested to Abraham's reliability in this area when He said, "I know him, that he will command his children and his household after him, and they shall keep the way of the Lord, to do justice and judgment." Abraham's experience with Ishmael gives me more hope than perhaps any other parenting incident in the Bible. Stung with the sorrows caused by his unfortunate marriage to Hagar, Abraham nevertheless taught Ishmael and modeled a godly life before him. After Sarah sent Hagar away, Hagar wanted to leave Abraham's values behind. Being an Egyptian, she sought an Egyptian wife for Ishmael. Ishmael wandered far away from the true God during his life, but his father's prayers followed him. "In his latter days he repented of his evil ways and returned to his father's God" (*Patriarchs and Prophets*, 174).

The unceasing pursuit of God's will

All of Abraham's life was spent in pursuit of this purpose: to obey the call of God as he understood it. With the first call, he uprooted his family from their ancestral tribe and friends in Ur. He left behind comforts and amenities in pursuit of an ideal, which God would, step by step, unfold to him. The pagan environment was left behind. With the second call, he left other branches of his family and departed from Mesopotamia, never to return. When famine struck in Canaan and there was no pasture for his flocks, he sojourned briefly in Egypt. But God called him to journey the length and breadth of Canaan, and he stayed as close to it as possible. Years later, when he sought a bride for Isaac, Abraham would not even consider taking a Canaanite woman for his son. He sent Eliezer and a caravan of camels back to Haran to find Rebecca, but he gave specific instructions that Isaac was never to return to Mesopotamia.

Abraham had cut with his past. He had been "called out" of his tribe, ancestry, and the comforts of one of the world's greatest civilizations. He had turned his back on them and made conscious, deliberate decisions to leave them and never return. His walk with the Lord became ever closer, until he talked with "the Judge of all the earth" face to face. He made mistakes, and his faith faltered, but he had turned his face toward Zion—there was no turning back.

Nahor, on the other hand, joined in Call number one, but would go no farther. Lot answered Call one and Call two, but only in a physical sense. Lot left Babylonia, but Babylonia never left him. He jumped at the opportunity to return to city life and its amenities and was willing to forfeit participation in Abraham's blessings, which never meant that much to him. Abraham daily renewed his heavenly citizenship at the family altar. There is no record that Lot ever built an altar or encouraged his family in spiritual sacrifice.

Hebrews, chapter 11—God's honor roll of those seeking the heavenly country more than an earthly one—dedicates more space to Abraham than to any other character.

By faith Abraham obeyed when he was called to go out to the place which he would receive as an inheritance. And he went out, not knowing where he was going. By faith he dwelt in the land of promise as in a foreign country, dwelling in tents with Isaac and Jacob, the heirs with him of the same promise; for he waited for the city which has foundations, whose builder and maker is God (Hebrews 11:9, 10, NKJV).

Seeking a Homeland

For your family

1. Do you know any people who have cut the ties with an old life, left it behind forever, and launched out into a new life? Discuss it with your group or family. Is it easier to make a geographical move or to make a spiritual change? Can you think of someone who changed locations for spiritual reasons? Share the story with your group or family.

2. In the news, we see and hear about brutal ethnic and tribal warfare. People are killed by the thousands for no other crime than being of the "wrong" ethnic group or political faction. Sometimes even "Christians" participate in these slaughters. Abraham was called to leave his ancestral tribe in order to follow God's plan. What would this mean in today's society? Are we first of all white Caucasians—or Christians? Blacks—or Christians? Americans—or Christians?

3. When Abraham moved, he built an altar. When moving into a new house, we can dedicate the house and establish family worship. The family can go through each room in the house, dedicate it to the Lord, and call upon the name of the Lord. They can let Satan know that the home and every room in it belongs to God.

4. God called; Abraham followed. The question is—Is God still calling us, and are we still following? What does God want me/us/our family to do? Am I willing to follow?

5. Idolatry was rampant in Mesopotamia and in Canaan. What are the idols in our family? Sports? Soap operas? Even doing good things instead of the best? When we put programs and things above God and above our family, the effect is to leave our children fatherless and motherless.

6. Are we doomed to repeat the mistakes and failings of our parents and grandparents?

To what degree does heredity determine our moral development? What does Ellen White mean when she says that the Holy Spirit has been given "as a divine power to overcome *all hereditary and cultivated tendencies* to evil"? (*The*

Desire of Ages, 671, emphasis supplied).

Do you know someone who came from an environment of low moral values but who chose to leave that past behind and to fulfill God's plan? Share the story with your group or family. If we belong to the heavenly Father, will we take on the Father's heredity?

Is it possible for parents to make right choices and start over again so their children, instead of sinking lower in the scale of spiritual friendship with God, can stand on their shoulders and reach greater heights?

4. What does it mean in the second commandment when it says "visiting the iniquity of the fathers upon the children unto the third and fourth generation of them that hate me; and showing mercy unto thousands of them that love me, and keep my commandments" (Exod. 20:5, 6, KJV)?

What meaning does it have to you if sins are transmitted to the third and fourth generation of those who hate God, but mercy is transmitted to a thousand generations of those who love God and obey Him?

Abraham received the promise that in you all the families of the earth shall be blessed (Gen. 12:3). Could your family be a blessing to all the families of the earth? How?

CHAPTER

7

GOING HOME OR SETTLING IN?

(John) Do you like to move? Our son John was in five different school systems during his first five years of school. Then the tide of our life changed; our family has had one address—the old home place—for the last twenty-five years. Some people are so rooted to where they live they would rather die than leave. Perhaps you remember the story of Harry Truman (not the former president) who lived on the side of Mt. St. Helens in Washington State. The mountain was smoking, the earth was rumbling, the forest service said "Move!" But Old Harry seemed to be part of the mountain, and he refused to leave. The volcanic eruption came. St. Helens blew its top. Old Harry is still there—now literally a part of the mountain.

Settling in—materially or philosophically?

At age seventy-five, Abraham was called to leave his country—to move. He was called to leave the comfort and convenience of Ur, one of the cultural centers of the world at that time, in exchange for a pilgrim life. As he followed the call step by step, God's covenant and promised blessings unfolded. Abraham's family traveled the land through its length and its width (Gen. 13:17) as strangers and pilgrims (Heb. 11:13). They sought a homeland; they desired a better, heavenly country (Heb. 11:14, 16). God blessed Abraham in his sojourn, with earthly riches.

Lot, Abraham's nephew, also came along. As long as he followed the divine commission to travel through the land, he also received the blessings. But the abundant blessings also brought a problem. Money at that time was largely counted in "sheep, goats, and cattle" (Gen. 13:5, TEV), and the land could not bear Abraham's and Lot's flocks. Was the basic problem material—or philosophical? Could it have been that Lot was looking for a change of lifestyle? He and his wife had enjoyed the comforts of the Mesopotamian cities. Why not settle in? Why all this moving from place to place, expecting a city which has foundations, whose builder and maker is God (Heb. 11:10) someday? From Lot's point of view, Abraham was to be pitied. Why "pie in the sky, by and by"? Wouldn't it show business acumen, foresight for the future, just plain logic, to settle in now?

The choice

Abraham offered Lot a choice of which way to go. In our geographical frame of reference, we might imagine Abraham looking north and saying, "Lot, choose whichever you like: to the right (east) or to the left (west)." However, the world of 1900 B.C. wasn't oriented north and south. Their maps had east, toward the rising sun, at the top. So, as Abraham looked at the central mountain range, he said, "Lot, the choice is yours. You take the right (north), and I'll take the left (south), or vice versa." Abraham hoped that Lot was going to stay in the mountain range, which ran north-south. But to live in the mountains represented a family commitment that Lot was not ready to make.

First of all, who had the right of choice? Years ago, when our family lived in South America, our children wanted to own a horse. The young woman who helped in our home had connections out in the country, and she sent a note with the bus driver ordering a horse for us. A younger worker who helped out in the office heard we had ordered a horse and decided he wanted one for his family, as long as we were ordering. So the next day, the young woman sent a second letter up to the hill country noting the order was now for two horses. We never thought much about the implications until about ten days later when two "gauchos" with their colorful vests and cowboy hats showed up in front of our house with two horses in tow. Just then the other worker came along, and we walked around sizing up the two animals. One was sleek and a beautiful brownish-red. The other was heavier and darker in color, with a little patch of white in the saddle area. Her name was "Sombra," or "Shadow." Now the problem arose: who was going to have which horse? Altruism is not natural to human nature. A battle was going on in my heart. One voice said, "You ordered the horse first. You are the older." The other voice said, "In honor giving preference to one another. . . . Whatever you want men to do to you, do also to them." The battle was intense. Family dreams of enjoying country life seemed to be at stake. But I forced myself to act from principle. "You choose first—we'll take the other one," I heard myself saying, almost against my will.

My colleague walked slowly around both horses, examining them in detail. Then he zeroed in on the sleek, beautiful, brownish-red one, patted her gently, and announced, "I'll take this one!" My heart fell. That was the one I had wanted! I have never been very successful in hiding my emotions. My wife knew how to read my face like an open book. She came over and whispered in my ear, "That's all right, dear. I like the gentle look in the eye of the dark horse." So we both paid for our horses, and my co-worker disappeared down the lane, taking my dream horse with him.

I can't tell you how much fun our family had with Sombra.

She was so gentle. In the morning, she would come to our window and softly wake us up. She would eat apples out of our hands. One of our prized family pictures is of both boys in the saddle with a cat and parrot, our two German police dogs looking intensely at the cat, my wife and I observing it all with pleasure in a special "zoo" family moment.

And the sleek, brownish-red horse? A few days later my co-worker announced he couldn't do anything with the animal. It seems he had chosen an ex-race horse—he didn't dare put his children on its back. I countered with "Oh, you just don't know how to ride him." Our family proceeded to go down to his place, and I prepared to mount the steed. My thoughts were, "All that is needed is a little rein and a strong hand." With me scarcely in the saddle, the horse was off like a shot. We seemed to be going sixty. I pulled back desperately on the reins but to no avail. The horse jumped a ditch and headed off across a tomato field. Eventually fighting him to a standstill, I dismounted with a "Thank You, Lord, for saving my life! Never again!" Sorry to say, the sleek brownish-red horse went to the glue factory—he also ended up in canned dog food. Letting others choose first is not necessarily a losing proposition.

Abraham was Lot's uncle, and according to the priority of the divine call—and by age—he had the right to make the first choice. When Abraham deferred to the younger Lot and graciously let him make the first choice, Lot decided to abandon the traveling lifestyle in the mountains and the continual dependence on God for water. The lush, green Jordan Valley looked so inviting. It offered economic insurance against dry spells. Uncle Abraham had always seemed kind of conservative and too careful in playing by the rules. Old Abe always spent so much time in worship and in building family altars. The deliberation was short: "Wife, daughters!" Lot announced. "We're going out on our own! We are going to strike it rich! Economic opportunity is knocking at our door!"

And Lot . . . pitched his tent toward Sodom (Gen. 13:12).

Going Home or Settling In?

Roger Babson, on country living

In the September 8, 1966, issue of *The Review and Herald* was an article by Ernest Lloyd entitled "Country Living." The author spoke of some correspondence he'd had some years before with Roger W. Babson, famed Wall Street analyst and investment adviser. Babson was so impressed with Ellen White's booklet *Country Living* that he ordered one hundred copies for his associates and friends. In a newsletter entitled "If Inflation Comes," Babson wrote the following to his clients:

> The purpose of this letter is not to advise you relative to stocks or bonds. Rather, my purpose is to emphasize that such are not the only or the best investments. In case of a real smash—which only a spiritual awakening can prevent—very few of the pieces of paper in your city safe-deposit box would probably be any good. . . . What Congress did in making us all turn in our gold and accept paper in exchange can easily be repeated and applied to all securities. . . .
>
> When you realize that most all the stocks and bonds in your city are in only a dozen or so vaults, which now are *under Federal supervision*, you can see how very easy it would be for Congress to take them away from us. . . . The chances are greater than four to six that you will see trouble.
>
> "All right," you say, "then what can we do about it?" I will tell you. *First*—we should develop character and health for ourselves and others. . . . It is utterly foolish to sacrifice one's character or health to save money. We should strenuously retain the health which we have and try to get back what we have lost. We should have a complete physical examination by trained diagnosticians once a year and follow their

advice as to habits, diet, and mental attitudes.

Second—we should spend money freely on devout teachers. . . . This means high-grade church schools and small colleges of the right character for our children. No amount of time and money is too great to spend upon properly educating and training children. . . . We should immediately begin to invest in them—to store up money *in children* instead of safe-deposit vaults.

Third—we should get a small subsistence farm upon which our family can spend at least their summers working. If possible we should not live in a large city. I really do not see much hope for city families. . . . For those not having a small farm, I especially commend high-grade summer camps. They are performing a very important service.

The safest way to save money is to turn it into character, health, and education. All other investments are very speculative, and this includes Government bonds, savings bank accounts, and insurance policies. Insurance companies will pay their policies in paper money, *but* what good will the money be? . . . The best insurance policy is a small self-sustaining farm and some good, husky, intelligent youngsters. . . .

Avoid large cities as you would smallpox centers. Large cities have caused the downfall of every nation which has thus far collapsed. Only a spiritual awakening can prevent the large cities of this country from falling into the hands of dictators, who by currency inflation and other means will try to rob the nation (*Review and Herald*, 8 September 1966).

Ellen White quotes on country living

"Fathers and mothers who possess a piece of land and a comfortable home are kings and queens"(*Fundamentals of*

Going Home or Settling In?

Christian Education, 327).

"Educate our people to get out of the cities into the country, where they can obtain a small piece of land, and make a home for themselves and their children. . . . Erelong there will be such strife and confusion in the cities that those who wish to leave them will not be able" (*General Conference Bulletin*, 6 April 1903, 87, 88).

"In God's plan for Israel every family had a home on the land, with sufficient ground for tilling. Thus were provided both the means and the incentive for a useful, industrious, and self-supporting life. And no devising of men has ever improved upon that plan. To the world's departure from it is owing, to a large degree, the poverty and wretchedness that exist today" (*The Ministry of Healing*, 183, 184).

"Again and again the Lord has instructed that our people are to take their families away from the cities, into the country, where they can raise their own provisions; for in the future the problem of buying and selling will be a very serious one. We should now begin to heed the instruction given us over and over again: Get out of the cities into rural districts" (*Country Living*, 9, 10).

For your family

Lot didn't intend to settle down in Sodom. But step by step, he moved his family in that direction, because the city offered a comfortable lifestyle and economic advantages. Sodom had a bad reputation: The men of Sodom were exceedingly wicked and sinful against the Lord (Gen. 13:13). Yet, apparently the advantages of city living meant more to Lot than the potential of participating in Abraham's blessings (Gen. 13:14, 15), and he was willing to risk the negative influence Sodom might have on his family.

1. Does Lot represent all of us, at least to a certain degree? Have we sometimes experienced that step by step we can get into a lifestyle, attitude, or behavior that we never

had intended to adopt? How does this process happen?

2. Lot was attracted by the economic opportunities and the abundance of water in the Jordan Valley. Maybe it tapped into a nostalgic longing he and his wife had for the cities in Babylonia they sometimes regretted having left.

Is there some temporal advantage that particularly attracts us?

Do we have a "price"? Would we be willing to modify our stance toward right and wrong if someone offered us a million dollars to compromise a little bit?

If we were to write out a list of our personal priorities or our family priorities, what would be first, second, and third on that list?

3. When Ellen White wrote her testimonies about the dangers of living in the cities and the advantages of country living, the ratio of the U.S. population was 90 percent rural to 10 percent urban. Today this ratio has flip-flopped, and the vast majority live in urban areas.

Are the counsels of Ellen White about raising our children in the country still valid? Has family country living been compromised by television? How can a suitable family environment be maintained for children?

In an age of agribusiness, when small farmers oftentimes don't survive, what economic arrangements could a family make to earn a livelihood and still enjoy the advantages of country living?

What might be the logical steps in transferring from city to country living? How long might this take?

If you live in a situation or culture where, in your present calling, you could not live in the country, what might you do to follow the principle behind God's instructions? Recently while in Moscow, we noted that the only housing available are monolithic high-rises, oftentimes twelve to twenty stories high. Housing is so scarce that several families may live together in a single room. In the spring and summer, families go to the country to their "dachas," live in temporary housing or little cabins, and raise the vegetables that will enable them to live in the winter.

4. Some families realize that the environment of their neighborhood is not conducive to Christian living. What are the options for these families?

5. Using the index to the writings of Ellen G. White, look up other quotations on country living. Study these as a family or group.

6. Have there been any warning signs in current events about the need to leave the cities?

7. What are your long-term objectives concerning country living?

8. What phased plan could you implement over a period of years to reach your objectives?

> Many are still making a similar mistake. In selecting a home they look more to the temporal advantages they may gain than to the moral and social influences that will surround themselves and their families. They choose a beautiful and fertile country, or remove to some flourishing city, in the hope of securing greater prosperity; but their children are surrounded by temptation, and too often they form associations that are unfavorable to the development of piety and the formation of a right character. The atmosphere of lax morality, of unbelief, of indifference to religious things, has a tendency to counteract the influence of the parents (*Patriarchs and Prophets*, 168, 169).

CHAPTER
8

THE LAST NIGHT OF SODOM

A Happy Lot
777 Dream Lane
Sodom

His was a smug satisfaction as he nailed up that sign on
the fence near the entryway.

Poor Old Abe, suffering out there on those desolate mountains! He heard his wife say, "Husband, the weather here is
so much better than in Haran, and this fine brick house you
built is infinitely nicer than our home was in Mesopotamia. I
never want to move again!"

As time went by, Lot became concerned about the language of the Sodomites. Some of the things he heard by the
city gate irked him. He didn't understand all the meanings,
but the lewd gestures of the locals, both men and women,
were coarse and seductive. Lot's daughters were attending
school in Sodom, and it seemed the local vocabulary was
beginning to rub off on them. When he remonstrated them,
they claimed they had been telling the other kids about the
true God and then went on to say something about the need
to adapt culturally in order to reach the people around them.

The Last Night of Sodom

Had his choice in moving to Sodom with his family been a good one? He wasn't sure. But he appeased his conscience by saying to himself, "The wife seems happier than I've seen her in a long time, and the balance in the bank account has never looked better."

Warning Signs

Warning Sign 1: Their daughters were getting into social life in Sodom and were beginning to date around. Lot held his head in his hands. What was that about the "holy seed" Abraham used to talk about? For a time, when Abraham had no son by Sarah, it had almost seemed probable that he—Lot—might become the promised heir. Now Abraham and Lot had separated, but this "holy seed" idea still bothered him. What if his children should intermarry with the Sodomites? Should he move away? Lot could not make up his mind to do anything radical, and besides, his wife claimed that the fellows the older daughters were dating really were pretty nice guys. No decision.

Warning Sign 2: For twelve years, Sodom and the surrounding cities had been paying taxes to Assyrian vassal kings who lived to the northeast. The thirteenth year, town meetings were stormy. The locals were tired of paying heavy taxes to foreign powers; they decided not to. In those times, to not pay your annual tax bill to a "protecting foreign government" was tantamount to a declaration of war. In the dry season of year fourteen, four powerful kings from Mesopotamia swept down to collect their bills, with interest. A sharp battle ensued. The king of Sodom, together with four ally kings, was outmaneuvered. The defending armies either fell into pitch pits, which abounded in the area, surrendered, or escaped to the mountains. The city of Sodom was plundered. Lot and his family became prisoners of war, and his extensive flocks were confiscated.

One of the survivors, probably one of Lot's hired servants,

escaped some forty miles to the west and informed Abraham of the tragedy. Abraham, usually a man of peace, armed 318 of his servants, together with a few men from three of the local chieftains, and pursued the army and captives all the way from southern Palestine past Dan in the far north—a distance of 150 miles. The contest seemed unequal: Abraham's servants against the vassals of the most powerful and cruel empire of the time, Assyria. But what Abraham lacked in manpower, he made up in superior strategy and—above all—his faith in God. In a sharp encounter, Abraham routed the enemy by night and on camels chased those who escaped to the region of Damascus, principal city of Syria.

The Bible says that when Abraham returned from the battle, he offered thanks to God and gave a tithe of all the loot to Melchizedek, priest of the Most High God. Nothing is said about Lot and his family feeling thankful.

The precarious moral, political, and family situation in Sodom should have spoken volumes to Lot. Was God trying to tell him something? Was Providence telling him he should take the bull by the horns and move out of Sodom while there was still time? But it would have been quite a decision to leave his real estate holdings and the lush green pastures of the Jordan Valley for the uncertainties of the mountains. The second warning to leave Sodom went unheeded.

Third warning—last call

It was the last night of Sodom. The day hadn't seemed that different from the thousand other days that had preceded it. People talked about trade, the economy, and loafed about enjoying the "good life." Toward evening, two apparently weary travelers came in through the city gate. Some of Abraham's good customs had rubbed off on Lot, and he approached the men and offered hospitality. When they answered that they would spend the night in the city square, Lot said, "Gentlemen, you don't know this place as well as I do. Things can get a little crude and violent around here. I insist that you find shelter under my roof and refresh yourselves with food at my table."

Even so, some contrasts appear between Lot's hospitality and that which Abraham had offered to these same guests a few hours before in Mamre. There, Abraham had outdone himself in gracious hospitality. He had sent a young man (possibly Ishmael) to prepare food, and Sarah had made some cakes. In Sodom there is no mention that Lot's wife or daughters participated in the hospitality at all. Maybe they had come to share the habits of Sodom. "Behold, this was the iniquity of thy sister Sodom, pride, fulness of bread, and abundance of idleness was in her and in her daughters, neither did she strengthen the hand of the poor and needy" (Eze. 16:49, KJV).

The supper was cut short as the inhabitants of Sodom gathered in front of the house and demanded that Lot send the two visitors out so the locals could abuse them by homosexual acts. For years, Lot had thought he could talk his way out of any jam. He had been long on talk and short on decision and action. He tried to parley with the corrupt men of Sodom, but his options were running out. Lot closed the door behind him. Perhaps he didn't want his visitors to hear his shameful offer of delivering his two remaining virgin daughters to the hoards outside for whatever sexual gratification they might desire, if the visitors would be left alone. What kind of solution was that to his problem?

Time and again, Lot, by his indecisiveness, had put others at risk. He put his wife and daughters at risk by moving to Sodom in the first place. He put Abraham and his servants at the risk of their lives when they militarily intervened in the surprise rescue of his family from the four vassal Assyrian kings. He put his family at risk again when he returned to live in Sodom in spite of the providential warnings. And now he put his daughters at moral and mortal risk to try to salvage a situation that seemed to have no good options. How had Lot gotten himself into such a corner? He seemed to have lost the virtue of decisive action. Instead, he had blended in with his environment, choosing the path of least resistance, doing whatever his wife and loved ones wanted him to do.

Lot was paralyzed. His visitors—angels—themselves acted. They physically pulled Lot into the house, shut the door, and struck the Sodomites with blindness. The doom of Sodom was pronounced, and the heavenly messengers unequivocally commanded Lot to take his family out of Sodom.

Lot rushed away to speak to his married daughters and sons-in-law. We don't know how many there were. There were at least two married daughters and possibly more. He felt that surely his years in Sodom had influenced some in the family toward the true God. Surely his sons-in-law would listen. He echoed the last call given by the angels: "Get up, get out of this place; for the Lord will destroy this city" (Gen. 19:14, NKJV). But unfortunately, Lot hadn't been a totally virtuous model himself, and nobody, nobody listened. The scripture continues: "But to his sons-in-law he seemed to be joking." His married daughters weren't listening either. Words fail to express the pain he felt.

A wretched, sleepless night passed. The remembrance of the laughter of his married daughters and sons-in-law still echoed in his ears. Must he leave his own flesh and blood behind? The grandchildren? What about his real estate and possessions? Must he leave everything? The Bible says:

> When the morning dawned, the angels urged Lot to hurry, saying, "Arise, take your wife and your two daughters who are here, lest you be consumed in the punishment of the city."
>
> And while he lingered, the men took hold of his hand, his wife's hand, and the hands of his two daugh-

ters, the Lord being merciful to him, and they brought him out and set him outside the city (Genesis 19:15, 16, NKJV).

The angels commanded them to escape to the mountains, but Lot still hesitated. "Not the mountains, Lord. We're really not mountain dwellers. Couldn't we go to this other nearby city? It is just a little city." Lot had never known how to submit to divine guidance—and still didn't yield implicit obedience. He would bargain, even on judgment day. But while he lingered and bargained, his wife turned to look at Sodom. What was in that glance? "My home. My children and grandchildren! My life!" If Lot had been decisive, his wife would have been saved. But joining in his vacillation, she looked back and disobeyed the direct command of the angel, "Escape for your life! Do not look behind you" (Gen. 19:17, NKJV). Lot's wife belonged to Sodom. Her heart was there. It was only fitting that she remained as a salty monument on the Sodom landscape.

Two thousand years later, Jesus said: "Likewise as it was also in the days of Lot: They ate, they drank, they bought, they sold, they planted, they built; but on the day that Lot went out of Sodom it rained fire and brimstone from heaven and destroyed them all. Even so will it be in the day when the Son of Man is revealed. . . . Remember Lot's wife" (Luke 17:28-30, 32, NKJV).

Archaeologists locate Sodom
On the east and southeast side of the Dead Sea in modern Jordan, archaeologists have identified ruins of five Cities of the Plain. The Bible lists them in the same order as the Ebla tablets excavated in Syria. Many archaeologists believe that the largest of these was Sodom, now called Bab edh-Dhra. Fifteen kilometers to the south was its smaller companion city of Numeira (Gomorrah). It is possible that the

Dead Sea did not extend as far south in the times of Abraham. Its southern terminus was possibly an extension of the peninsula that now juts out into the Dead Sea. (Today a barrier has been extended at this narrow point across the sea, and the walled-off area serves as the location for mining various minerals found in the evaporated sea deposits.)

Sodom was located near the northern point of this peninsula. Bab edh-Dhra had a walled area of at least ten acres and a large settlement outside the walls. The city wall averaged seven meters in width and was made of stone and mud-brick. Houses were built of fine brick, rectangular in plan, and averaged about five meters in length and two or three meters wide. Walter E. Rast (*Archaeology*, January/February 1987) estimates that perhaps a minimum of six hundred people lived in the walled city and perhaps an equal number lived outside the walls. The city was supplied with water by Wadi edh-Dhra and Wadi Kerak (a "wadi" is a stream). Supposedly, the scarcity of water mandated that instead of building one large city, the population spread out to satellite cities located on other wadis. The inhabitants of Gomorrah buried their dead at Sodom. The ruins show evidence of earthquake activity and also show that the city was destroyed by a conflagration. There is evidence of severe burning on many of the stones, and the area is covered with spongy ash. Bitumen (asphalt or flammable petroleum substances) abounds in the area of Sodom. It sometimes comes to the surface of the Dead Sea in large globs. There is evidence that the area was formerly well wooded, although now it is barren and desolate.

For your family
    1. As a family or group, discuss some of your good and bad choices and the consequences of those choices. Discuss the importance of good choice-making.
    2. What does Lot's story say to us about last-day events?

The Last Night of Sodom

When last-day events start moving rapidly, how might God direct our family as to where we should go or what we should do?

3. In what areas of life are we doing what family members expect us to do? What if you are impressed to do differently? Do you impose your will? Do you follow the majority vote? Do you pray and work the matter through?

CHAPTER

9

TROUBLE EN ROUTE

Disappointments. Frustrations. Questions. Confusion. We do not like them. But for some reason, God sends them—or at least permits them to come—our way. We have been told that if we did not have some "fiery furnace" experience our characters would never reach their true beauty. While in the furnace of affliction, we sometimes wish it would be all right if our characters were only ninety percent beautiful. But the reason we are in the furnace is that we all have a problem called earthliness. Like an evil tree, we have roots of selfishness that run far deeper than do our mere overt sins. We have what family counselor Larry Crabb calls a fallen structure in our human personality. We may have clipped the leaves and pruned some unsightly branches as society has demanded or as God has led us. But the evil root is still there.

From the diary of a wanderer
"I enjoyed being pampered by my mother; I deceived my father, and ended up striking a hard and crooked bargain with my older twin brother. When that exasperated brother threatened to kill me, my worried mother sent me away to the land she had come from, hoping I'd be beyond the reach

of my brother's arrows. (He was a bullseye marksman in archery!)

"But now I'm trying to do the right thing, Lord. So why am I getting into trouble? I want to go home. I have set my heart on it. Now Esau is coming my way with an army of four hundred men, apparently bent on revenge. God, I know I thought in that dream at Haran that You told me to come back home. And the other day at Mahanaim, I saw two bands of angels guarding us, one in front of us and the other protecting us to the rear. But if You are calling me to go home, and I am obeying Your Word, why are Esau and four hundred of his men coming to kill me?"

Past blessing, yet a root problem

Jacob accepted God and asked that the blood of the coming Saviour cover his sins. He knelt at the family altar with Isaac. He heard the story of the sacrifice on Mt. Moriah— *Yahweh-Jireh*, The Lord will provide Himself an offering (Gen. 22:14). Jacob had his Bethel experience and saw the vision of the ladder uniting earth with heaven—and the angels of God ascending and descending on it. He set up his pillar and made his vow. He worshiped humbly and said, "Surely the Lord is in this place, and I knew it not."

But in spite of all those indications of God's overriding guidance in Jacob's life and of God's acceptance, there was still something missing. He had deeply rooted tendencies— sin[1] as contrasted with *sins*—that he had never dealt with. How could God get through to him on a deeper level to claim not just part of Jacob's mind but his whole heart? God decided to get Jacob's attention.

God talk

"Jacob, your testimony before the world is still a mixed message. You have been a deceiver since you were a child. You deceived your father, Isaac, in the question of the birthright. I know that you say your mother told you to do it, but you were responsible. You weren't a child—you were seventy-seven years old! I know you had waited for over half a century, and you were afraid that your blind old father was failing and might not ever get around to giving you the blessing the angel promised you at birth. But you weren't willing to let Me work out the question of the birthright in My own time and in My own way. You thought that since I seemed to be slow, you would have to take things into your own hands.

"Life has had a way of paying you back. You deceived Isaac, and Laban deceived you. He tricked you and gave you the wrong wife on your wedding night. You bargained for wages after working off the dowry for fourteen years, and Laban changed your wages ten times. I've revealed Myself supernaturally to you three times[2] in your life, but the old Jacob is still there. Deep, deep down, you still have character flaws that are keeping you from knowing Me as I would like to have you know Me. You haven't fallen on the rock and been broken. There has always been something superficial about our walk together.

"So this night before Esau is due to arrive to massacre you and your wives and children—this night on which you have broken your camp into two so that if he slaughters one group the other may have some chance to escape—we have some business to attend to. We need to talk."

Trouble

Trouble upon trouble, an unknown assailant attacked. Jacob was no slouch when it came to physical fitness. He had fought with wolves and lions to protect Laban's flocks and his own. He brought all his brute force to bear in the contest. It was a battle! The Bible calls it wrestling. Maybe it was wrestling with no holds barred. It was a battle for survival, and there was no one who could help him. The struggle continued hour after hour, supported only by the flow of adrenaline that kept Jacob from utter exhaustion. Somehow, even his greatest exertions were insufficient to conquer his enemy or to cause him to abandon the battle. In the loneliness of his struggle, a picture of Jacob's life came up before him. For years he had been fighting; he had been his own worst enemy. "We have met the enemy—and it is us!" How could he expect victory from God in returning home when deep in his heart, he had never made a clean break with his past? The old habits were like weights chained around his feet, like mire that impeded his progress. He needed victory not only in his current battle; he needed it over every besetment, over every sin in his life.

The dark night was passing; the sky was beginning to brighten in the east. For hours the attacker had used only human strength in the struggle. Thinking that his opponent was a human enemy, Jacob had fought for his life with all his brawn and muscle. But as the dawn approached, just one supernatural touch sufficed to cripple Jacob. He was almost incapacitated with pain as his hip slipped out of joint. Who had he been fighting with? It was God Himself. The Divine Being spoke: "Let me go, for the day breaks." But, clinging to Him in all his pain, Jacob exclaimed, "I will not let You go unless You bless me!" He longed for the greatest of blessings—forgiveness and a new character.

For years, Jacob had wanted to reach out and touch God. Now he had God in his grasp, and He refused to lose that opportunity. He chose to claim the blessing of a completely transformed character that had eluded him even during the twenty years of wandering from his father's house. At that moment, he was more concerned about his own relationship and knowing God than he was with the ominous threat of Esau and his four hundred sword-carrying warriors.

God spoke: "Jacob, for more than twenty years I've been trying to get through to you and talk to you about your soul. What is your name?"

"Jacob," is the puzzled response.

With deep kindness and love, God answered, "Your name will no longer be *Jacob* the deceiver. That is the old man you used to be. You are now a new man. I Myself give you the name *Israel* or *Prince With God*, for you have struggled with God and with men, and have prevailed." The scripture adds "and he blessed him there" (Gen. 32:29, KJV).

Wrestling with God

Why all the wrestling? Why all the trouble? The answer is earthliness. We all claim to be citizens of heaven, but much of the earth has fastened on us all. We claim to be *in* the world and not *of* the world, but the world is too much with us. Our sins have been forgiven. God knows they have been many. The slate is clean, covered by the blood of Jesus. But the tendencies behind those sins are so hard to change!

What does the Time of Jacob's Trouble have to do with last-day families? The families who live to see Jesus coming will go through an experience typified by Jacob's night of wrestling with the Angel. "For thus saith the Lord; We have heard a voice of trembling, of fear, and not of peace. . . . All faces are turned into paleness. Alas! For that day is great, so that none is like it: it is even the time of Jacob's trouble; but he shall be saved out of it" (Jer. 30:5-7, KJV).

"Jacob's night of anguish, when he wrestled in prayer for deliverance from the hand of Esau . . . , represents the experience of God's people in the time of trouble" (*The Great Controversy*, 616). As Jacob's family approached home, unarmed and defenseless, they seemed about to fall as helpless victims of violence and slaughter. Jacob realized that it was his own sin that had created their danger. In the long hours of the night, he interceded with God, confessed his sin, and claimed the promises of the covenant made to his fathers and to him in the night vision at Bethel. This was the crisis of his life. Everything was at stake. He wrestled with his old self. He wrestled with the Angel and finally clung, helpless and weeping, to the neck of his mysterious assailant. "He had power over the angel, and prevailed" (Hosea 12:4, KJV). So it will be in the end time of trouble, as believing families and as individuals we will plead with God for deliverance. The death decree will have been signed. All human protection will have been removed.

> The season of distress and anguish before us will require a faith that can endure weariness, delay, and hunger—a faith that will not faint though severely tried. The period of probation is granted to all to prepare for that time. Jacob prevailed because he was persevering and determined. His victory is an evidence of the power of importunate prayer. All who will lay hold of God's promises, as he did, and be as earnest and persevering as he was, will succeed as he succeeded. Those who are unwilling to deny self, to agonize before God, to pray long and earnestly for His blessing, will not obtain it. Wrestling with God— how few know what it is! How few have ever had their souls drawn out after God with intensity of desire until every power is on the stretch. When waves of despair which no language can express sweep over the suppliant, how few cling with unyielding faith to the promises of God (*The Great Controversy*, 621).

The new Jacob, the new you

The sun rises in Gilead. As the camp wakes to a new day, a lone figure crosses the Brook Jabbok. The man limps painfully into camp. Yet there is a glow on his face, an assurance and peace. He is a new man. His name is no longer *Deceiver*; he has wrestled with God over his past and conquered. He is no longer afraid of what man might do to him. Let Esau come—he has nothing to fear. God is completely in charge of his life and has given him an assurance on which he builds his hope. Now he can say, "I'm ready to go home, because home is already in my heart."

For your family

1. "Mark the perfect man, and behold the upright: for the end of that man is peace" (Ps. 37:37). Looking truthfully into your hearts, are trials something you see as ways of perfecting you and your family? Share some of your trials with your group or family. What positive effects did they have on your family or on you?

2. James Audubon spent years painting beautiful pictures of birds in the woods. When he finished his work, he carefully put all his pictures in a wooden crate, nailed it shut, put it under a bed for safekeeping and left to attend to some business. Upon his return, he discovered that rats had nested in the crate and destroyed all the paintings.

If you had been James Audubon, how would you feel? What would you do? Discuss this with your family or group.

The blood rushed to James Audubon's head. It seemed he could not think. After a time during which he truly grieved, his tremendous sense of loss subsided, and he said: "I will go again into the woods, and I will paint better than I did the first time!" After a year, the work was done—more beautiful than before. The results are the classics that were ultimately published and are still treasured as priceless.

3. What earthliness do you have as a family that needs to be given up before you go home?

Have you been dealing with any deep-rooted tendencies that may have run in the family for years, or have you glossed them over, saying they are just part of the family heritage? The hereditary chain linking the evil traits of grandparents, parents, and children can be broken. However, this will take deliberate identification of the problem areas and specific claiming of God's promises.

Trouble en Route

If you were to ask God to help you wrestle now (before the Time of Jacob's Trouble, when it will be too late) with one besetting sin, what would it be?

Are you prepared to accept that struggle?

Take time to reevaluate your journey. Ask for forgiveness for each area of sin; be assured of that forgiveness. All you must do is ASK for forgiveness. It is that simple. The struggle may not end; in fact, it may intensify. But it is not the struggle that is sin. You may fall, but Christ's forgiveness allows you to get up without looking backward. God is the Giver of help and strength and is the bondage breaker. He gives VICTORY! Satan wants us as captives, but Jesus wants to give us freedom. As we wrestle with God over past sins, we, too, can conquer.

4. Prayer

"Lord, I choose You as Lord and Saviour of my life and desire to serve You and keep Your commandments. I acknowledge that I am a sinner and desire forgiveness of my sins. I ask you to reveal to me the sins of my life by the Holy Spirit. Show me where I have given ground to Satan and where I am in bondage.

"I am sorry for _____ and ask You to forgive me for this sin. Other sins are _____. I truly am sorry for the pain I have caused You and others and now repent of these sins.

"I know that I have been deceived by Satan and reject him and reclaim any ground given to him, and I want him to depart from me and my family. Give me victory. You paid the price for me on the Cross, and through You I can be free. I believe You have forgiven me and will help me to be an overcomer.

"Help me daily to put on the whole armor of God (Eph. 6:10-17) and to be firm in my spiritual life and be able to resist the devil. I realize that I am a part of the battle between good and evil. I choose the good—the true—and reject evil and Satan's deceptions. I ask that You send the Holy Spirit to be with me as I go on this spiritual journey with

You. Jesus, I want Your mind and heart, and I know You will never leave me nor forsake me.

"Lord, You have forgiven me, and I no longer need to feel guilty for my sins. I thank You for this freedom.

"Now, Lord, show me whom I need to forgive—those who have hurt me. They are _____ . I also pray the "foot of the Cross" prayer for them: Forgive them, for they knew not what they did to me. I forgive them now, and I know that You will help me to process these painful memories. I choose to forgive, and I don't want to hold on to this bondage any longer. I want freedom in forgiveness for myself and _____.

"I now pray that if I have hurt someone, that You will bring it to my attention so that I can make it right with them. (It may be a family member.) Give me the courage to make it right. Let nothing separate me from You and Your great love. I pray this prayer in the powerful name of Jesus, who died on the Cross for my sins. Amen."

As a family, discuss this prayer, and then suggest that each individual have a quiet time to reflect on the prayer and pray as the Holy Spirit directs. Add praise to the Father, the Son, and the Holy Spirit, as well as thanksgiving.

5. Jacob, the "Deceiver," was victorious and became Israel, "Prince With God." In the rest of the Bible, God calls Himself "The God of Abraham, Isaac, and Israel." The people of God are called "the children of Israel." The twelve tribes who stand in victory on the sea of glass are named after his twelve sons. Wow! Lord! If You can do this for an old deceiver, what are You going to do for me?

---

1. *Sin* is independence of God. "I will be a Christian, but I will do it my way." This root tendency gives rise to many overt thoughts and acts that are *sins*.
2. The three times were the dream at Bethel (Gen. 28:12-15), the dream at Laban's place where God commanded him to return to the land of his family (Gen. 31:3, 11-13), and at Mahanaim where two camps of angels met him (Gen. 32:1, 2).

CHAPTER

10

FAMILY SEALED BY BLOOD

The last-day family that overcomes will go through one last midnight trial. What will it be like? Words are inadequate to describe that awesome experience, but history records one midnight hour 3,500 years ago that foreshadowed the last night that awaits us. Exodus 12:42 calls it the "night of the Lord."

The plagues

One by one, the terrible plagues had fallen on Egypt, aimed at objects of false worship and at a lifestyle separating the people from God. Water had turned to blood. Frogs by the millions had invaded the land. Lice had caused itching on men, women, children, and beasts. While idolaters suffered under the ever-deepening scourge, God's true followers had been protected from the plagues. Clouds of flies swarmed over the land, buzzing, bothering, and biting those who didn't fear the Lord. God drew a clear line between the true and the false. The cattle that had been worshiped as gods fell strangely ill and died. The ashes of a furnace (symbolizing the furnace of slave affliction) were sprinkled toward heaven, and the fine-falling particles produced painful boils on all creatures—humans included. Hail devastated property the wicked had accumulated by forced labor of God's people.

"We will go with our young"

Pharaoh was willing at last to give limited freedom to some of the people, but he wanted the children left behind. Today, the enemy sometimes concedes that particular individuals have been freed from the shackles of sin, but he is most anxious that whole, intact families not go together out of the oppression of sin into freedom. Why? First, he doesn't want the united testimony of parents and children in a world where he has insisted that marriage and parenting don't work. Second, he knows that when a house is divided, the believing ones will not have the human support that would encourage them to be faithful. Who will go forth out of Egypt? Today we would ask, Who is being called forth out of Babylon? Moses answered in Exodus 10:9, "We will go with our young and with our old, with our sons and with our daughters." "Let my people go" (verse 3). Now, as then, God yearns to have whole families—fathers, mothers, children, in-laws, grandparents, infants in arms, youth in their strength, and the elderly in their rich experience—leaving the world behind and going home together. "Tell in the hearing of your son and your son's son the mighty things I have done . . . that you may know that I am the LORD" (verse 2, NKJV).

A plague of hail followed the boils, smashing hoarded materialism and showing the hollowness of a religion calculated to appease the powers of nature. Then a supernatural darkness covered the land for three days, symbolizing the spiritual darkness of a people who had refused to know the Lord. The king and his subjects, still unrepentant, were next visited by the plague of locusts, which finished devouring the crops their idol gods were powerless to protect. But the greatest lesson of all was reserved for the experience of the tenth and last plague.

God has always claimed children as His own property. Parents may feel that their children belong to them. Some state governments, by laws and coercion, in effect, claim children are theirs. While all children belong equally to God, in the Old Testament He sought to establish His ownership early in the family life cycle by setting aside the firstborn particularly as His treasure. Parents who acknowledged God's ownership and their stewardship over the first fruit of the womb would doubtless continue to recognize their stewardship of God's gifts in other children who would grace their home. God hoped to teach in one momentous lesson the only way our children can be saved for the kingdom of heaven.

Safe under the blood

Moses and Aaron announced before the children of Israel, and then before the king of Egypt, that at midnight the death decree would be executed upon firstborn who were not protected by blood. The children of Israel were given minute specifications on how their families could be preserved. Each family was to slay a lamb and, with hyssop brush, put some of the blood on the two doorposts and on the lintel of their houses. A roasted lamb was then to be eaten by all those in the family.

With the chores and packing completed, the family lay down to sleep. Eliezer, the oldest son, found himself staring into the darkness. Soon his voice whispered, "Daddy, is the blood on the doorposts?"

"Yes, son," came a sleepy reply, "Don't worry. The blood is on the doorposts."

An hour later, after a fitful sleep, Eliezer called again into the darkness, "Daddy, Mommie—are you *sure* the blood is on the doorposts?"

Wakening again, his father responded, "Son, I told you the blood is on the doorposts. Our servant Jehu took care of it. Go back to sleep."

At almost midnight, young Eliezer woke with a start. "Daddy, Mommie, are you *absolutely sure* the blood is on the doorposts?"

His father stumbled across the room, took the hand of his beloved son, and in the shadowy darkness they made their way together to the door. It was just moments before midnight. A full moon shone over the Goshen landscape. There was the basin, the hyssop, and—*where was the blood mark*? Had the servant been so busy with the preparation for the Exodus that he had forgotten? Hands trembling, Eliezer's father seized the hyssop and frantically spattered the blood on the doorposts. Seconds later, anguished wails arose in the darkness from houses whose entryways were without blood. Except for the land of Goshen, not a home escaped. Death's angel visited all: from the firstborn prince of Pharaoh in the palace to the firstborn of the servant who worked in the field.

The Passover has a few unforgettable lessons for us. The feast introduced that night was to commemorate the deliverance from Egypt, but more important, it was to be an illustration of the way Christ would free His people from the bondage of sin. The lamb represented "the Lamb of God which taketh away the sin of the world." It wasn't enough that the lamb be slain—its blood must be sprinkled on the doorposts. It isn't enough that Christ died on Calvary. The merit and assurance of that sacrifice must be applied in the life of the home, most beautifully in family worship. Family worship claims the hope of the shed blood of Jesus and covers families through Christ's blood, safe from the onslaught of the enemy. Hyssop is like a natural broom—this symbolized cleansing. The psalmist says, "Purge me with hyssop, and I shall be clean; wash me, and I shall be whiter than snow" (Ps.51:7, NKJV). The lamb whose blood stained the doorposts was to be eaten. It is not enough to believe theoretically in Christ as our Saviour. He longs to become part of our being. We are not just spectators of the Christian hope—we are to be participants.

In the *Review and Herald*, September 19, 1854, Ellen White said, "The seal, or mark, of believing parents will cover their children, if they are trained up in the nurture and admonition of the Lord." Today the destroyer is stalking the land. Only those with the mark or seal will be protected.

How do we put the blood on the doorposts? Every morning, noon, and night, parents should place the lives of their children in the hands of God, claiming the merits of Christ as their assurance. The husband/father, as priest of the household, has the first responsibility to do this. He should claim the redeeming blood for his spouse, and together they should claim the blood for their children. Throughout the day, let fathers, mothers, and children send "dart prayers" to God's throne for each other, claiming deliverance through the blood of the Lamb. This will thwart the plans of the enemy.

Ellen White says:

This experience of the Israelites was written for the instruction of those who should live in the last days. Before the overflowing scourge shall come upon the dwellers of the earth, the Lord calls upon all who are Israelites indeed to prepare for that event. To parents He sends the warning cry: Gather your children into your own houses; gather them away from those who are disregarding the commandments of God, who are teaching and practicing evil. Get out of the large cities as fast as possible. Establish church schools. Give your children the word of God as the foundation of all their education. This is full of beautiful lessons, and if pupils make it their study in the primary grade below, they will be prepared for the higher grade above (*Testimonies for the Church*, 6:195).

For your family

1. One mother said that when she discovered the wickedness that existed outside the doors of her home, she could not allow her child to leave the home without having spiritual protection around and over her. God honors the prayers of parents and sends angels to guard their children in their daily activities. But parents must ask for this angel protection.

2. Develop a collection of Bible verses for family worship that are especially meaningful for you. For starters, we suggest two:

Psalm 91:7, 10: "A thousand may fall at your side, and ten thousand at your right hand; but it shall not come near you. . . . Nor shall any plague come near your dwelling" (NKJV).

Revelation 12:11: "And they overcame him by the blood of the Lamb, and by the word of their testimony; and they loved not their lives unto the death."

As a family, begin to collect verses, discovering how they apply to your own unique difficulties. Make them your own.

3. Prepare a sacred Family Covenant and pledge to each other that you will, by God's grace and strength, be faithful to God and to each other through good times and bad times in the cosmic controversy between good and evil. After all family members have signed the covenant, enshrine it in your family museum of memories. Renew the covenant at least every seven years* in a special ceremony, perhaps at a family reunion.

4. Discuss as a family the importance of individual and

family worship and how you as a family can make it more spiritually meaningful as well as powerful.

---

* The Israelites were to read and renew the covenant with their families every seventh year at the Feast of Tabernacles (Deut. 31:10-13).

CHAPTER
11

ALMOST THERE

"For of all sad words of tongue or pen
The saddest are these: 'It might have been!' "
—Whittier

(John) In April of 1846, the Donner party started out from Illinois by covered wagon to make their new home in northern California. On July 20, Donner led twenty wagons onto the untried Hastings Cutoff around the south side of the Great Salt Lake. Equipment broke down, and their progress was slower than had been projected. Tortuously, they wound their way up the rugged trail. On October 31, they arrived at Truckee Lake, high in the Sierras, the last chain of mountains that separated them from the fertile valleys that would be their home. Snow began to fall. Soon the pass was blocked. Hemmed in by many feet of snow, the group could go neither forward nor backward. Facing starvation, seventeen of the strongest men attempted to cross the Sierras on snowshoes in December. Seven of them survived. From January to April, four relief parties rescued the remaining survivors. Only forty of the eighty-seven emigrants ever made it home across the Sierras, away from what is today known as Donner Lake and Donner Pass.

Our hearts go out to the people whose eager footsteps wanted to go home, who bent every effort toward home, and who, only because of forces beyond their control, didn't arrive. At least home was in their hearts, and many of them died with the hope of a better land where someday they would find an eternal home. However, there was another group of people who journeyed well for a while. They said they wanted to go home. Everybody thought they were headed in that direction. Then something mysterious happened—some deceit, some strange love, some bewitchment came over them, and they didn't go home after all. Paul spoke of this kind of people when he wrote: "You ran well. Who hindered you from obeying the truth?" (Gal. 5:7, NKJV). "O foolish . . . ! Who has bewitched you that you should not obey the truth?" (Gal. 3:1, NKJV). "Let us therefore fear, lest, a promise being left us of entering into his rest, any of you should seem to come short of it" (Hebrews 4:1, KJV).

Baal-peor
For forty years, the children of Israel wandered in the desert. Most of the elderly had died, but many who were under twenty when they left Egypt were still alive. Well over a million others had been born after the Exodus. There had been trials along the way: Amalek pounced on their rear guard; with God's intervention, the Israelites won the day. They had conquered Moab, and Sihon, a giant, who was king of the Amorites. How many blessings they could tell their grandchildren! The falling manna and the stream of water that came forth when Moses struck the rock had followed them through the wilderness. For years they had been protected from the scorching sun by a cloud by day, which turned to a soft light at night so the camp would not be in total darkness (Exod. 13:21, 22). They had seen the cloud over the sanctuary—proof of the presence of the living God.

And there they were, camped on the plateau of Moab. Below them wound the silvery Jordan, and beyond was the Promised Land. The trip was almost over. There was the land promised to their fathers, flowing with milk and honey! Stretching off to where the horizon met the blue sky were forests, orchards, and fertile fields. They were going to inherit that land—land that would hear their children's laughter. They had come an interminable distance, and now they were almost home!

Satan's most successful plan

On the very border of that Promised Land, Satan launched a counterattack. Balak had tried to curse these Israelites, but every time his hired prophet Balaam spoke, he pronounced a blessing instead of a curse. He could not curse those whom God had blessed. So long as they were faithful to God, there was no power in hell or on earth that could stop them from conquering Canaan and entering into the rest for which all them had longed for so many years. As his first plan was not working, the wily Balaam came up with a different strategy: "Balak, you have some lovely young women. Have them mix seductively on the outskirts of the camp. Let them interest the men in a little romance, a bit of enticement, and hopefully a great deal of sex. After all, it's been a long trip in the desert—not much entertainment. Encourage them to let themselves go and have a good time!"

We will not enter into unnecessary details. The Bible tersely reports:

> And do not become idolaters as were some of them. As it is written, "The people sat down to eat and drink, and rose up to play." Nor let us commit sexual immorality, as some of them did, and in one day twenty-three thousand fell" (1 Cor. 10:7, 8, NKJV).

Almost There

Think of it—23,000 transgressed the seventh commandment and died by God's judgment in one day. They never got home.

Satan's last ploy

As the people of God, we have come up again to the borders of the Promised Land. Long we have wandered in the deserts; now but a moment of time remains until Jesus comes in the clouds of heaven. This time, it is not an earthly Canaan we hunger for. We are one step from the heavenly Promised Land. Satan is unleashing his final strategy. Ellen White has warned us of the final temptation the enemy will seductively employ to induce even the mighty to fall:

> As we approach the close of time, as the people of God stand upon the borders of the heavenly Canaan, Satan will, as of old, redouble his efforts to prevent them from entering the goodly land. He lays his snares for every soul . . . ; he will prepare his temptations for those in the highest positions, in the most holy office; if he can lead them to pollute their souls, he can through them destroy many. And he employs the same agents now as he employed three thousand years ago. By worldly friendships, by the charms of beauty, by pleasure-seeking, mirth, feasting, or the wine cup, he tempts to the violation of the seventh commandment. . . . Those who will dishonor God's image and defile His temple in their own persons will not scruple at any dishonor to God that will gratify the desire of their depraved hearts (*Patriarchs and Prophets*, 457, 458).

No one is immune to the temptations of the flesh. We don't hear people speak so much anymore about committing adultery and fornication. Today society uses less judgmental terms: an affair, a midlife crisis, a fling, a one-night stand. Sins we once loathed are slowly tolerated and finally embraced. Immorality and infidelity are the characteristic sins of today. These sins attack children, youth with their exploding hormones, and those of maturing years. My mother used to say, "There is no fool like an old fool!"

Some years ago on one of our trips overseas, we learned of the case of a man who had been a most successful Christian worker. In his older years, he became infatuated with a younger woman. He was so blinded by lust that he was willing to sacrifice his wife of thirty years, his three children, his ministry, and his employment. He was quoted as saying that this relationship was so wonderful that if it meant giving up heaven, he was willing to do it. Strange infatuation! Mystery of iniquity!

Satan is, indeed, very serious. But praise God, we need not fall. We can learn from the sad experience of the past.

> Now all these things happened to them as examples, and they were written for our admonition, on whom the ends of the ages have come. Therefore let him who thinks he stands take heed lest he fall. No temptation has overtaken you except such as is common to man; but God is faithful, who will not allow you to be tempted beyond what you are able, but with the temptation will also make the way of escape, that you may be able to bear it (1 Cor. 10:11-13, NKJV).

When Satan presents his seductive temptations, we can answer him, "It is written, Thou shalt not commit adultery or fornication. Get thee behind me, Satan!" Don't listen to Satan's enticing invitation to sexual evil. Strongly, loudly, rebuke Satan. Pray for God's strength to be faithful and chaste. Claim God's promises and run from evil.

To look at Jesus is to see His matchless purity and concern, which would never exploit another's weakness or degrade another who is a child of the King. Jesus is cheering you forward. On life's journey, you've gone through a thousand trials and given your life to Jesus, claiming citizenship in another land. You have run the race well for a time. You could be an encouragement and good example to another weary traveler. You could say with the poet, "My strength is as the strength of ten, because my heart is pure." Would it be worth it to cast it all away for the fleeting pleasures of this world, when you're almost home?

For your family

1. It is commonly thought that if young couples live together for a time before marriage, they are more apt to stay together after marriage. Do you think this is true? Discuss. After everyone in the group has given their opinion, read and discuss the following:

Jeffry Larson, marital therapist from Brigham Young University, has assessed all the most recent literature about couples living together before marriage. He says: "Almost all studies show a higher divorce rate for those who cohabit than those who do not. One study shows up to a 50 percent greater chance [of divorce]" *(USA Today*, 10 May 1995, 1D).

2. How can one keep from getting caught up in the "sex-mania" of the media today? Make a list of spiritual principles one can follow that will keep himself/herself pure.

3. The psalmist asks the question, "How can a young man [woman] cleanse his [her] way?"(NKJV). Read Psalm 119:9, 11 and discuss whether this will still work in the world of today.

Dr. David Seamonds, a noted Christian psychologist, in his tape series on temptations—"The Way of Escape"—says that the best way not to fall into temptation is to use preventive measures. For some youth, in their own strength, the temptation of immorality may seem almost overpowering.

However, we may "immunize" ourselves to a great degree against these temptations by having an active prayer life, by daily enjoying the power of the Holy Spirit, and by a faithful study of God's Word. Temptations that might have swept us away may never affect us, because we have avoided the environment associated with that temptation. The affections of our hearts have been dedicated to the Lord, and we walk in safe paths. This is *prevention*.

However, God does not shield us from all temptation. The very object of trial is to prepare us to resist all the allurements of evil. The story of Joseph and Potiphar's wife illustrates this. When, in the line of duty, we are confronted by enticement, we can realize that we are in the presence of God, not just the seducer. With Joseph we can say, "How then can I do this great wickedness, and sin against God?" (Gen. 39:9, NKJV). In the moment of crisis, we can close our eyes to blot out every other view or thought and silently pray, "Jesus, help me now!" This is *intervention*. "Neither wicked men nor devils can hinder the work of God, or shut out His presence from His people, if they will, with subdued, contrite hearts, confess and put away their sins, and in faith claim His promises. Every temptation, every opposing influence, whether open or secret, may be successfully resisted" (*The Great Controversy*, 529). God would sooner send every angel from heaven to the help of sincere souls than see them fall under the power of the enemy.

Sometimes we have fallen to temptation. The Christian should keep short accounts with God. When we fall, there is no need to do penance, to wait days or years to claim forgiveness. We may immediately flee to Christ, immediately confess and repent, ask His pardon, and claim His covering blood. John writes, "My little children, these things I write to you, that you may not sin. And if anyone sins, we have an Advocate with the Father, Jesus Christ the righteous" (1 John 2:1, NKJV). "For a righteous man may fall seven times and rise again" (Prov. 24:16, NKJV). This is not to belittle sin. Sin pains the heart of God and leaves scars and consequences. But thank God, when we go to God in prayer, He will hear us, cleanse us, and put us on the right path again. This is *intercession*. God's plan to give us victory over temptation is beautiful and complete. *Prevention, intervention, intercession*. What a wonderful Saviour!

4. As a family, discuss sexual temptation and sexual abuse and give sexual instruction to your children. If you don't, someone else will. And you as parents may not like the instruction.

Remind the younger generation that they can report sexual abuse to legal authorities.

Instruct the children against strangers' advances. Instruct them against sexual advances by relatives.

Discuss with teens and older ones the importance of being chaste. Teach them how to be assertive and say, "No, I am a virgin and choose to remain this way until marriage, as is God's plan. Take me home."

Memorize promises that are powerful over the tempter, such as: "Fear not, for I am with you; be not dismayed, for I am your God. I will strengthen you, yes, I will help you, I will uphold you with My righteous right hand" (Isa. 41:10, NKJV).

Discuss how Satan will give suggestions to the mind and the importance of saying, "I reject your temptation, Satan." Don't listen to Satan's deception that says illicit sexual activities are love. They are not love. They are lust and are evil and wrong.

Discuss: As Christians, we should not do anything in the dark that we would be ashamed to do in the daylight.

CHAPTER

12

HOW FAR FROM HOME?

How often have parents heard this question from the back seat: "How long till we get home?" Children seem to feel that since we're going, we should be able to get there *now*. In life, when we are doing something pleasurable and having fun, it seems as if time has wings—the hours fly by as if they were minutes. But when there is unfulfilled desire in the heart, it seems as if the minutes are hours, the hours are days, and the days are years. Our computers used to seem fast when they were twenty-five or fifty megahertz in speed. But now the sky seems to be the limit. When we have to wait a few seconds for the computer, it seems painfully slow.

Yet time passes relentlessly, knowing no haste and no delay. Events that seemed long postponed finally come to pass. We were holding family evangelistic meetings in Moscow. Our immediate task was formidable, and our responsibility was taxing. There were pressing family concerns at home. Millie's mother figure, who raised her from the age of nine when both her parents died, was failing, and although we comforted ourselves in that she was receiving the best of care, we wanted to be at her bedside in our home attending her. It seemed as if the fly-home date would never come. But it did, and we were able to return to our loved one and her needs. We are so thankful we spent the last three weeks of her life beside her and were able to comfort her on the last night of her life with song and Bible promises of hope. And then the end of her fourscore years and ten came, timed just right by a loving heavenly Father so that we could give the memorial of her life quality time, unhampered by conflicting appointments.

In our personal lives we have found it almost uncanny to see answers to our prayers for continual divine guidance. We have seen God schedule momentous events according to His own timetable, and everything has gone like clockwork! All this has strengthened our full confidence in our Lord, and with the psalmist we can say, "My times are in Your hand" (Psalm 31:15, NKJV), even when, to our eyes, some of God's timings seem painfully wrong and without explanation.

How long?

If this is true on a personal level, how much more sure it must be on a world and cosmic scale. How comforting it is to know that "like the stars in the vast circuit of their appointed path, God's purposes know no haste and no delay" (*The Desire of Ages*, 32). Yet the time seems long. Bible prophets and persecuted saints over the millennia have asked again and again, How long, Lord, until You do something? (Ps. 74:9; Dan. 8:13; Rev. 6:10). God declared to Abraham that after a period of 400 years of sojourn, the children of Israel would come out of bondage. All the might of the most powerful nation on earth battled in vain to keep this from happening, but when the divine clock struck, "on the self-same day" they came out of Egypt. Almost a millennium later, God's people were again in captivity, this time in Babylon. The prophet Jeremiah had foretold a captivity of seventy years. God had to overthrow the first world kingdom to bring it about, but when the divine clock struck, God's people were free to come out of Babylon.

Recently, we have been reading several excellent

Seventh-day Adventist books published on the Second Coming. Marvin Moore's *The Crisis of the End Time* and G. Edward Reid's *Even at the Door* are significant and informative reading. We have been blessed and informed by both these and other works. We are impressed with the strong lines of argument presented that show that the atmosphere—the religious-political perspective as a setting for end-time events—is awesome. The pieces of the jigsaw puzzle are coming together. The stage seems to be set—which is something we could not have said with such evidence even five years ago.

While it is not necessary we all agree on every detail (and I for one don't want to join the ranks of the date-setters), it is sobering to see that the players in the final drama seem to be in place. G. Edward Reid submits the interesting proposition that while God's people could and should have hastened the coming of the day of the Lord, God has set outside limits beyond which He will not wait. Realistically, if the coming of the Lord depended on our efforts and the present rhythm of the work, then taking into account the population explosion, Christ would never come. However, we know that "it will be seen that He [God] is taking the reins in His own hands" (*Evangelism*, 118), and that "He will finish the work and cut it short in righteousness, because the Lord will make a short work upon the earth" (Rom. 9:28, NKJV). *Even at the Door* goes on to expound evidence from J. N. Andrews (*Review and Herald*, 17 July 1883), one of our ablest early theologians, that even before Adam and Eve had sinned, God's great clock gave Lucifer and his angels a week of millennia to prove their government better than God's own. There would be six thousand years of rebellion and one thousand years of judgment to encompass the great controversy, and after this had finished, time would again blend into eternity.

Warren Johns, SDA Seminary Librarian, states that there are forty-four six thousand year statements published in Ellen White's primary sources before her death in 1915. In ten of these, she used the qualifier *nearly* or *almost*, in three she used *about*, in four she used *more than* or *over*, and in twenty-seven she used no qualifier, but simply stated six thousand years. In addition, there are forty-two statements which refer to a period of four thousand years between Creation and the first coming of Christ. These four thousand year statements cannot be used to establish an exact chronology because some of them would conclude at Christ's birth while others carry forward to Calvary. Available chronological data is insufficient to justify stating with precision when six millennia since Creation week might have concluded or will conclude. However, it is abundantly clear that we are living at the end of the sixth millennium. Like the prophet of old, we can confidently proclaim, "Repent, for the kingdom of heaven is at hand!"

In the chapter "The Family's Last Call," we present evidence that the end-time Elijah message coincides with the pre-advent judgment beginning in 1844 (Mal. 4:5, 6; Mal. 3:1, 2; *The Great Controversy*, 424, 426). While the "Messenger of the covenant" is pleading for us in the temple in heaven, "My messenger" (those who are represented by Elijah) will be doing a work on earth. Great events in heaven call for corresponding great events on earth. There is nothing more powerful than an idea whose time has come. The hearts of fathers and mothers will be turned to their children, and the hearts of children will be turned to their parents.

God's great family clock

On page 205 of *Even at the Door*, G. Edward Reid presents a clock chart of all Earth's history from Creation to the second coming of Christ. The twelve-hour face of the clock equals six thousand years, each hour equals five hundred years, and each minute equals one hundred years. In this chapter, we have adapted this diagram and called it God's Great Family Clock. It deals with the scope of this present book and shows highlights of the family and the call back home in salvation history.

Let's examine history at a glance on the face of our clock. For the sake of illustration, we will look only at the hour hand as it makes a full sweep around the clock from noon to midnight. The twelve hours from noon until midnight equal six thousand years. Each hour represents five hundred years, and each minute represents one hundred years.

Let's place some noteworthy family events on our clock. Most of our numbers have been rounded off, since our purpose is the big sweep of events and not to make an exact chronology. At Creation, God instituted His ideal for marriage and the family. This has never changed. Adam lived until almost 2:00. Meanwhile, Enoch walked with God for three hundred years, and his son Methuselah lived until 3:00 and died the same year that Noah and his family were saved in the ark. Abraham was called out of Mesopotamia at 4:00 (about 1875 B.C.), and the promise is given that in him all the families of the earth will be blessed. Meanwhile, Lot barely heeds the last call out of Sodom but loses his family for the kingdom. At 5:00, the children of Israel are called out of Egypt in the Exodus (about 1445 B.C.).

David is the midpoint of human history at 6:00 (1000 B.C.). Soon after, Elijah on Mt. Carmel calls Israel out of idolatry and into "heart turning." God's children go into captivity and are called out of literal Babylon at 7:00. A century later (430 B.C.), Old Testament prophecy closes with Malachi's Elijah end-time call. The greatest events of salvation history come at 8:00. John the Baptist announces Christ's first coming and calls for "heart turning" and the restoration of all things (Matt. 17:11-13). Jesus lives and dies, making the salvation of every believing family secure by the merits of His blood. By 9:00, we've come to the fall of Rome and the establishment of the papacy. At 10:00 (1000 A.D.) we've come to the mid-point of the Dark Ages. The Waldensian persecution follows, and at 11:00 the Reformation breaks forth.

Now comes the exciting part. In 1798, which is approximately two minutes till midnight, the "time of the end" begins—a date point in prophecy. Now the end events can begin to unscroll. In 1844, with our clock lacking approximately one minute thirty-four seconds till midnight and counting, the judgment hour begins in heaven. Great events in heaven call for corresponding great events on earth. The final Elijah restora-

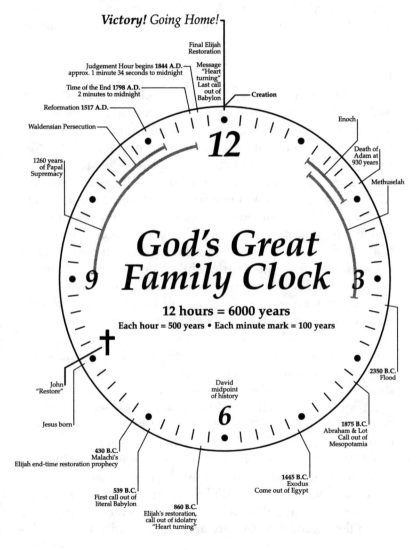

Victory! Going Home!

Final Elijah Restoration

Judgement Hour begins **1844 A.D.** approx. 1 minute 34 seconds to midnight

Time of the End **1798 A.D.** 2 minutes to midnight

Reformation **1517 A.D.**

Waldensian Persecution

1260 years of Papal Supremacy

Message "Heart turning" Last call out of Babylon

Creation

Enoch

Death of Adam at 930 years

Methuselah

God's Great Family Clock

12 hours = 6000 years
Each hour = 500 years • Each minute mark = 100 years

12

9

3

6

2350 B.C. Flood

David midpoint of history

John "Restore"

Jesus born

430 B.C. Malachi's Elijah end-time restoration prophecy

539 B.C. First call out of literal Babylon

860 B.C. Elijah's restoration, call out of idolatry "Heart turning"

1445 B.C. Exodus Come out of Egypt

1875 B.C. Abraham & Lot Call out of Mesopotamia

tion message is given on earth, calling for "heart turning" repentance, and God's people are given the last call to come out of Babylon. Where are we today? Only seconds until midnight. The great controversy is almost over. Our clock started with Creation, and it will make the complete sweep to a new creation. There will be victory and total restoration. Our family *will* be going home!

When will Jesus come?

We have not attempted to set a precise time for the Second Coming. We are interested in the cadence of the events and the big picture. To us, the most striking part of the picture is that it puts our much-discussed problem of the "delayed advent" into perspective. Seen from the viewpoint of God's great clock and the twelve hours of great controversy history, approximately one minute thirty-four seconds isn't very long. "Therefore do not cast away your confidence, which has great reward. For you have need of endurance, so that after you have done the will of God, you may receive the promise: 'For yet a little while, and He who is coming will come and will not tarry' " (Heb. 10:35-37, NKJV).

We don't know the exact date of Creation. The genealogies don't permit us to establish a precise chronology. Apparently, God in His wisdom has seen fit to leave the question too ambiguous for time-setting precision. We do know that some four thousand years passed between Creation and the birth of Jesus. Was it exactly four thousand years? We don't know. The birth of Christ must be placed before the death of Herod the Great. Authorities place the date variously between 6 B.C. and 4 B.C. When we don't know something exactly, it would be safer to say it was approximately four thousand years. So much for the past.

How about the future? Will the earth's history be six thousand years of sin, followed by a Sabbath that corresponds to the millennium? Ellen White and pioneer Adventist theolo-

How Far From Home?

gians such as J. N. Andrews state this. The analogy is to the seven-day week—six days of human activity followed by a seventh day of rest. Is the analogy meant to be interpreted with precise dates? Since we don't know precise dates for either Creation or the birth of Christ, it would seem prudent to be careful not to predict an exact future date based on them. When we don't have an exact starting point, it is difficult to state unequivocally an exact ending point.

Another question is: Are the six thousand years themselves *exactly* six thousand years? Some things of the past have happened with great precision. Exodus 12:40, 41 states that the children of Israel lived in Egypt for four hundred and thirty years. "At the end of the four hundred and thirty years—on that very same day—it came to pass that all the armies of the LORD went out from the land of Egypt" (NKJV). Will the end of the six millennia be that precise? Many scholars, basing their arguments on the Egyptian kings list, believe the earth is already more than six thousand years old. We do not know. Again, maybe prudence would suggest that we would be safer to speak and write in terms of *approximately* six thousand years. However, when we get to heaven, and all the dark has been made plain, and the whole picture is seen in cosmic perspective with all the historical evidence in, we just may be surprised to see how beautifully it all fit together.

We believe that the King is coming *very* soon. We want to be like the wise men who, even from an ambiguous prophecy like Balaam's—"A Star shall come out of Jacob; A Scepter shall rise out of Israel" (Num. 24:17, NKJV)—upon seeing the star, were ready to go meet their Redeemer-King. We want to be like John the Baptist who, from his wilderness sanctuary, "with awed yet exultant spirit . . . searched in the prophetic scrolls the revelations of the Messiah's coming,—the promised seed that should bruise the serpent's head; Shiloh, 'the peace giver,' who was to appear before a king should cease to reign on David's throne. Now the time had come. A Roman ruler sat in the palace upon Mount Zion. By the sure word of the Lord, already the Christ was born" (*The Desire of Ages*, 103).

The players for the last great drama are in place. We would not cheapen the final act by insisting that it follow our interpretations of its schedule. Some may try to electrify us by predicting the *eschaton* in the year 2,000. But danger lurks in date-setting. Some may imagine they show faith by "proving" a date in what seems to them to be the near future, only to discover that their preparations were too far postponed and the Master returned sooner than they expected. The curtain of the heavens is about to open for the final scene. We shall see the King in His beauty! Good news! We're seconds till midnight. The family is going home!

For your family

1. If you have not accepted Jesus as Lord of your life, and if you want to be part of God's kingdom and go to the heavenly home, please pray this prayer:

Heavenly Father, today I choose Jesus Christ as the Lord of my life. I reject this world as my real home. I want to go home with You and live throughout eternity with You. Forgive me for my sins _____ _____, and change me to be more like You. I pray that the Holy Spirit will come into my life. Please work through the Spirit and perform Your miracles in my life. Lord, I want to go home with You— I know You are waiting for me. In Jesus' name, Amen.

2. While we are waiting, what are some things God encourages us to do?

A.

B.

3. What evidence do you observe in the world that indicates Christ is coming soon to take us home?

CHAPTER

13

SKELETON IN THE FAMILY CLOSET

(Rated "PG": Parental guidance suggested. Parents would need to adapt this story if used for young children.)

She wasn't a bad woman, judged by those times. On the other hand, neither could she be considered virtuous. Her vocation? A prostitute—the only life she had known since adolescence. In fact, part of the ritual of leaving childhood had been to go to the temple of the moon goddess to offer her body to any man who desired it. In her culture, sex was considered a worship tribute to the moon goddess. The more sexual relations a woman had, the more religious she was.

The female deity that protected her city had several names, including Asherah. In the legends of her people, Asherah was portrayed as the lover of Baal, a male god that was the rider on the clouds, bringing rain and good crops. Her city was one of the oldest cities in the world, and these religious customs had been practiced as long as anyone could remember.

All the men she knew were much the same. Their only interest was to exploit her. Sometimes she felt more like a thing than a person. However, this kind of life was economically profitable, and in time she managed to acquire a boardinghouse that took in travelers who were passing through and with whom she could ply her trade.

In her heart of hearts, she longed for something better than her way of life, with its selfishness, greed, and violence. Some nights when there was a full moon, people would gather in the temple and offer babies as sacrifices. It seemed so contrary to even the natural affections of motherhood. If only there were another god of love and justice instead of this goddess of exploitation and violence.

Two strangers

Late one afternoon, two men came into town and asked for a room for the night. They seemed to have a peace and kindness about them when they came down to the dining room for supper. After everyone else had left except the two strangers, the woman's curiosity finally got the best of her. She asked, "Why are you so different from other people?" Here were strangers who treated her like a person instead of a thing. At first they were reticent to answer, but little by little they opened up and told her about the God they worshiped. Her eyes brightened as she heard about a God who loved people and who was the Creator of earth and sky. In fact, according to the two strangers, God had created her and wanted to give her strength to live a life of dignity and worth.

The darkness of night had settled over Jericho, but by the light of an oil lamp she could still see the two men's faces as she whispered, "I would like to know your God and worship Him. I want to leave my old life behind." The lamp flickered and grew dimmer as they talked on in subdued whispers into the early hours of the morning. She learned that her city was doomed to destruction. The God of heaven could bear with Jericho's injustice and violence no more. Tears came into Rahab's eyes as she said, "My father and mother, brothers and sisters, are in this city. Like me, they are searching for a better way of life. Does the God you worship show mercy on those who are willing to forsake their past and live for Him?"

The truth begins to dawn on the two strangers. They thought they had been sent to Jericho only as spies. They had not realized until now that God had sent them there as missionaries. Their mission was not just to smite down but to call out. "We worship a God who forgives. In fact, our rituals teach us that God Himself will come down to earth and shed His blood so all who accept Him may be saved," they answered. "Rahab, a few days from now when Jericho will be destroyed, we want you and your family to be saved. Look, there on the wall you have a coil of scarlet cord. That color reminds us of the scarlet blood of our coming Saviour. If you will hang that scarlet cord from your window on the wall, we promise you by the honor of the God of heaven that you and your family will be saved."

The "rest of the story"

The walls of Jericho fell down except for a section where a scarlet cord hung from a window. Enshrined forever in the faithful hall of fame are these two verses:

"By faith the walls of Jericho fell down after they were encircled for seven days. By faith the harlot Rahab did not perish with those who did not believe, when she had received the spies with peace" (Hebrews 11:30, 31, NKJV).

Rahab never returned to her old life. After she and her family were rescued from Jericho, she fell in love and married a fine Hebrew man by the name of Salmon. God blessed them with a son, and their great-great-grandson's name was David. And maybe you've heard of someone else in the family. Her great-great-great-great-great-great- . . . (we ran out of ink to write all the "greats") great-grandson—Jesus!

For your family

We recently conducted a Marriage Commitment Seminar where in a women's group, one woman shared how her life had been traumatized and almost ruined by abuse from her father when she was a child. Another woman shared the following with the group: "I was sexually abused as a child. I know the pain that comes from being exploited and used. I took this pain to the Lord. I finally realized that I had a choice. I could live in the past and remember day by day and hour by hour the hell I suffered, or I could say, 'The past is past. I don't have to live there anymore. I *can* get on with life.' "

1. On our journey home, circumstances of life haunt us. Mistakes have been made, but God is a very merciful God who forgives. We will never find God by denying who we are and where we've been. We need to move *through* our problems to find God, not just move *around* in denial and also not *into* them to the point where the past controls us in the present. Give examples of biblical stories that show how God's loving grace and forgiveness empowered people to change their lives:

-David

-Mary Magdalene

-

-

Discuss these stories as a family, looking for concrete examples of our assurance that God sees us as we can be—not just as we are in light of what has happened to us or what we have done.

2. Sometimes we try to find God while we are totally engrossed and absorbed in our own problems. But if the in-look is depressing and the outlook is bleak, why not try the up-look? Although we may have ongoing struggles with such things as low self-esteem, scars from sexual abuse, and loneliness—all part of Satan's arsenal—we can look up to God, and our very sense of need can be used to draw us into a closer relationship with Him. This is one of the greatest beauties of God—that even out of Satan's worst evils, God assures us of hope. Out of the wreckage of our lives, He will

build a precious palace fit for eternity.

Carefully—and without resorting to easy answers—discuss as a family how this is possible. Seek to encourage each other in the process.

3. There are many times when professional Christian counseling can and should be sought. Discuss this with your family, helping all members to realize that there is dignity and strength in seeking out wise counsel.

4. Have you ever been sent on a mission and, as a serendipity, you sensed that God had used you in some way that you had not even expected? Share your story.

5. How might someone who had Christian upbringing in reality be worshiping the goddess Asherah?

6. Parents, discuss the importance of reporting when a person touches someone in their private areas.

CHAPTER

14

BLOODSTAINED CHOICES

(Rated "PG": Parental guidance suggested. Although true, the violence of this story may not be appropriate for young children.)

We don't know the story of her husband. It could have been that he died in an accident or that he went to war in those troubled times and never came back home. What we do know is that this unnamed woman was left with seven sons. It may seem strange, but there were no daughters. The life of a single-parent mother trying to raise seven sons is not easy today, and it wasn't easy then. There were no government agencies to appeal to—and no charities. One had to do the work of two. One had to be all—supporter, worker in the fields, nurturer.

If grieving could have brought back a lost mate, hers would have returned years ago. But somehow in life, she must leave the past in the past. Today had sufficient tasks to demand all her attention. And then, of course, tomorrow—what would become of her seven sons? Would they grow up in the fear of the Lord? Would they be an honor to God and to their country? All she could do was to invest sixty seconds of character into each minute of distance run. She would teach her sons to be truthful, to obey the laws God had given their ancestors, and to be loyal to that God—whatever the cost.

Even in the best of economic times, life would have been rough. But as long as she could remember, her homeland had been the scene of war, famine, and bloodshed. Her little country had the bad fortune of being located between two superpowers. Whether the power to the north invaded the kingdom to the south or if the south invaded the north, the result was oftentimes the same. Devastated fields and rape and beatings from the armed forces were commonplace.

The crisis*

It was the year 168 B.C. The king of the superpower to the north, the Seleucids, or Syria, decided on an all-out attack on the superpower to the south, the Ptolemies, or Egypt. A huge war machine of tens of thousands of chosen troops marched through the tiny buffer state of the Holy Land, led by the king of Syria himself, Antiochus Epiphanes. His name meant "Antiochus the Brilliant, or the Shining One." His capital, Antioch, was the scene of glorious display. His lavish lifestyle and the banquets he threw for his officers and foreign officials were legendary. He had an enormous ego and spent money like water to gratify his every whim. He was already more famous than any who had preceded him in the kingdom. Rumor had it that he hated the Jews with a passion. Fortunately, it was the Ptolemies of Egypt who currently were top on his hit list.

Antiochus proudly led his vast army to the borders of Egypt, only to be met there by an official, the legate of Rome. "Antiochus," demanded the legate, "turn around and return to your country. If you take one step into Egypt, the legions of Rome will invade Syria on the western front." The decision was a difficult one for the haughty king, but regretfully the infantry, the cavalry, and the engineers with their mammoth battering rams, portable towers, and boulder-hurling engines turned and began to wind their way back north.

Antiochus the Shining One sulked like a child. What could he do to cover his humiliating retreat? Perhaps you have heard the story of the man whose boss humiliated him. He couldn't do anything against the boss, so he came home and took it out on his wife. The wife didn't know how to get back at her husband, so she took it out on their son. The son didn't know how to get back at his mom, so he went and kicked the dog. All this misplaced hostility because Dad had a rough day at work! That's what happened with Antiochus. Except he took it out on the Jews.

Arriving in Jerusalem, he banned worship of the true God, Yahweh. He sacrificed pigs on the temple's altar of burnt offering to make his point. He next decreed that all Jews must give up their religion or be butchered. The Sabbath must be profaned. Idol shrines were set up, and people were forced to offer incense on them. Women who had their children circumcised were put to death, with their babies hung around their necks. Thousands capitulated to the pagan rites, while the faithful few were thrown into a crisis fully as critical as when Hezekiah faced Sennacherib, as when the three Hebrew worthies were thrown into the fiery furnace, as when Queen Esther and all other Jews were ordered to be killed. Antiochus's purpose was genocide. He would exterminate the Jewish nation and religion.

A family choice

Having accomplished his will in Jerusalem, the king moved with detachments of soldiers out into the cities and towns. He soon arrived at the village where the single-parent mother of our story lived with her seven sons. The local population was rounded up by the rough soldiers and herded into the presence of the king. Perhaps thinking that this single parent with her seven dependent children would be easier to influence than others, the king tried to force them to taste pork by torturing them with whips and scourges. One of the sons, acting as spokesman for the others, protested and said, "We are prepared to die rather than to break the laws of our God." The king's face turned red in fury at this answer, and he ordered that pans and cauldrons be heated over a fire. When these were red-hot, he had this son's tongue cut out, his head scalped, and his extremities cut off. Then he brought the youth—still breathing—and had him fried alive in the pan. In emotional agony, his family comforted themselves with God's promises and asked Him to take pity on His servants.

The second son was brought forward next. Skin and hair were ripped from his head, and he was then admonished to eat some pork or his body would be tortured limb by limb. His answer was No! He, too, was tortured. He, too, died.

The third son was tortured next. On being asked for his tongue, he thrust it out and held out his hands saying, "Heaven gave me these limbs. For the sake of His laws I have no concern for them. From God I hope to receive them again." The fourth was subjected to the same torments. As he died, he said: "Ours is the better choice, to meet death at men's hands, yet relying on God's promise that we shall be raised up by Him."

The fifth bravely met death in his turn, followed by the sixth. Meanwhile, the mother encouraged each of them in their ancestral tongue and said, "I do not know how you appeared in my womb. It was not I who endowed you with breath and life. The Creator of the world made each of you. He in His mercy will give you back breath and life."

From the tone of their voices, Antiochus suspected that the family was insulting and ridiculing him, though he could not understand the Hebrew tongue. He would force any and all to honor his word as law. He approached the youngest child with promises to make him rich and give him public office if he would abandon the traditions of his ancestors. Since the boy seemed oblivious to the king's words, the king appealed to the mother, urging her to advise her youngest son to save his life. Bending over her only remaining child, she said: "My son, have pity on me. I carried you nine months in my womb and fed you at my breast three years. I fed you, reared you, provided for you. Do not fear this executioner, but prove yourself worthy of your brothers and accept death so that I may receive you back with them in the day of mercy."

The mother had scarcely finished, when the young man answered the king with resolution, "What are you waiting for? I will not comply with your ordinance. I will obey the law given by God through Moses. My brothers have endured brief pain and for the sake of ever-flowing life have died for the covenant of God. I, too, like my brothers, surrender my body and life for the laws of my ancestors, begging God's mercy upon our people." Antiochus Epiphanes was outraged at this testimony and tortured the youngest even more cruelly than the others. The mother was the last one to die after her seven sons. They were together in life and were not separated in their death. Together they will rise in the resurrection.

Loyalty in this last generation

Today, on the verge of the second coming of Jesus, families are also faced with choices. They may not seem as dramatic as those faced by a single-parent mother and her seven sons some 2,100 years ago. Yet subtly, day by day, we are choosing whether we will obey God or man. If we do not obey God in times of peace and prosperity, how will our families be prepared to obey Him when the death decree hangs over our heads?

The revelator says of the overcoming throng: "And they overcame him [Satan] by the blood of the Lamb and by the word of their testimony, and they did not love their lives to the death" (Rev. 12:11,NKJV).

"Choose poverty, reproach, separation from friends, or any suffering rather than to defile the soul with sin. Death before dishonor or the transgression of God's law should be the motto of every Christian" (*Testimonies for the Church*, vol. 5:147).

For your family

1. What trials do we have today that will make us strong tomorrow?

2. What are the things we can do when unjustly treated that will help us through difficult times? Please be *very* specific. Think of actual, *real* trials and difficulties and *concrete* responses.

3. All of us have pain—often deep pain—from past injustices done to us. God longs to free us from this pain so we can live fully. Consider the issues you may have that need healing. Are you willing to begin the path of working through those problems? Even if it means seeking professional Christian counseling? God offers freedom, not denial. And God offers a tearless joy—and a strength-filled eternity.

4. Life is not fair, but God is. Discuss this concept with your family or group.

5. Those who don't stand for something will fall for everything. Discuss this concept with your family or group.

---

*The story is based on 2 Maccabees 7:1-41. This book makes up part of the Apocrypha and is accepted as a part of the Catholic Bible. Most Protestants do not accept this book as inspired and as a part of the sacred canon. However, it is an historical account of the stormy years of the Maccabean Revolt, beginning about 168 B.C., which led to an independent Jewish state for about a century during the intertestamental period.

CHAPTER

15

THE BLOODSTAINED PATH

"IN TENEBRIS LUX"
("INTO THE DARKNESS, LIGHT")
Waldensian Motto

An individual and family pilgrimage

Our travel toward the kingdom of heaven is oftentimes pictured as an individual journey. Take John Bunyan's classic *Pilgrim's Progress* as an example. We traveled to Bedford, England, and found Bunyan's birthplace, after searching in country wheat fields. In the Bunyan Museum, we saw the wicket gate after which he patterned part of his story, and in Bedford we saw the parsonage of the minister who brought peace to Bunyan and after whom he modeled Evangelist in the allegory. There is a sequel to the classic that speaks of Christiana, Christian's wife, who also follows the road to the Celestial City. Our children were raised on *Little Pilgrim's Progress*, and now the same worn book is captivating our grandchildren. So children must also make the journey and fight the battle of faith.

While there is undoubtedly an individual dimension to the heavenly journey, we are concerned here with trying to capture the family dimension in leaving the City of Destruction and going home together to the Celestial City. Few epics in history have portrayed this family journey more aptly than have the Waldensians, when families prayed together, studied in their homes, and sent out their youth as missionaries into a world thirsting for their blood. Ultimately, thousands of families died. They were together in life, were together in death, and will be together at the glorious return of our Lord Jesus Christ.

We journeyed to the valleys of the Piedmont in northern Italy to gather information and to try to catch the spirit of these indomitable Christians who for more than eight hundred years suffered and survived, passing on to their children the true, unsullied gospel light. We arrived in Torre Pellici, Italy, during the days when the Waldensians were celebrating the three hundredth anniversary of their "Glorious Return," when, using guerrilla tactics, they had fought their way across the Alps from an unjust exile and reinstituted their homes and their way of worship in their native valleys.

From the days of the apostles, God has always reserved to Himself a faithful remnant of whom the world was not worthy. While nominal Christianity descended into the darkness of apostasy, here and there were a faithful few who remained uncompromised to Rome. The beginnings of the Waldensians are shrouded in some mystery. Ellen White speaks of their witness for the ancient faith during the Middle Ages "for a thousand years" "behind the lofty bulwarks of the mountains." To this torch, kept burning and passed on oftentimes by unnamed hands, the Waldensians fell heir (according to their own historians) around the year 1170. By the early 1200s, they were multiplying in the mountain valleys around Turin in northern Italy.

The Waldensian family

The center of Waldensian economic, social, and religious life was the home. This occurred partly because in the early movement there was not sufficient wealth to build churches and also because persecution forbade public meeting places. But, perhaps most important, the home became the activity center through the sacredness of family ties and because of the primary need to pass on the heritage of their way of life to their children. Their clandestine meeting places were in their home and at times in subterranean caverns of the mountains.

It was in the home the parents taught their children. Into the home, the Waldensian leader and pastor, the *barba*,[1] came to instruct youth and to encourage family piety. The family functioned as an economic unit and also as the transmitter of sacred spiritual trusts. This was accomplished through an emphasis on Scripture, which was internalized through close family relationships as they joined ever closer for survival in a world where the government and the church were united in a desire to force them to recant or die.

Let us visit a fourteenth-century Waldensian home to taste this atmosphere and observe it in action. We gather with the family at a rough-hewn table and bow our heads as the father, or the mother in his absence, says grace: "May the God who blessed the five loaves and two fishes for His disciples in the desert bless this table and its provisions." Then, before eating, we all join in repeating the statement of belief and the Lord's Prayer, finishing with the sign of the Cross. The meal of simple food is eaten with warm conversation, centering on spiritual and practical topics. After the meal, we all stand, link hands, and lift our eyes to heaven as the leader repeats from Revelation 7: "Blessing, and glory, and wisdom, and thanksgiving, and honor and might be unto our God forever and ever." And finally, "May God bless all who do good, bless us with material and spiritual food, and abide with us."[2] Simple? Yes! But daily, these truths were being etched indelibly into the hearts and lives of all members of the family.

The Bloodstained Path

What values were taught in the home?

The location of their homes itself was a constant lesson. Here were parents who chose to rear their children in the mountain fastnesses instead of among the works of man. The outdoor sanctuary of awful grandeur befitted the great truths committed to their trust. The mountain valleys in which they lived were surrounded by towering heights that spoke to them of the unchanging majesty of God "with whom there is no variableness nor shadow of turning, whose word is as enduring as the everlasting hills" (*The Great Controversy*, 66).

In family priorities, understanding and doing the will of God took first place. "The principles of truth they valued above houses and lands, friends, kindred, even life itself. These principles they earnestly sought to impress upon the hearts of the young" (ibid., 67).

Peter Waldo had early translated the Bible into the French dialect of the people. A principal Waldensian activity was to copy portions of Scripture. Copies of the Bible were rare, since movable-type printing was still centuries in the future. If anyone was found carrying portions of the Bible, it could mean death or imprisonment. This lent urgency to the memorization of large portions of both the Old and the New Testament. Many youth memorized the books of Matthew and John. From earliest childhood, the youth were instructed in the Scriptures and taught to regard sacredly the claims of the law of God. Emphasis was on the Sermon on the Mount and practical religion rather than on the hair-splitting theological arguments of the time.

Parents—as the principal teachers—associated the thoughts of God with the sublime scenery of nature and with the humble blessings of daily life. Little children learned to look with gratitude to God as the Giver of every favor and every comfort.

Ellen White says:

Parents, tender and affectionate as they were, loved their children too wisely to accustom them to self-indulgence. Before them was a life of trial and hardship, perhaps a martyr's death. They were educated from childhood to endure hardness, to submit to control, and yet to think and act for themselves. Very early they were taught to bear responsibilities, to be guarded in speech, and to understand the wisdom of silence. One indiscreet word let fall in the hearing of their enemies might imperil not only the life of the speaker, but the lives of hundreds of his brethren. . . .

From their schools in the mountains some of the youth were sent to institutions of learning in the cities of France or Italy, where was a more extended field for study, thought, and observation than in their native Alps. The youth thus sent forth were exposed to temptation, they witnessed vice, they encountered Satan's wily agents, who urged upon them the most subtle heresies and the most dangerous deceptions. But their education from childhood had been of a character to prepare them for all this. . . . Their garments were so prepared as to conceal their greatest treasure—the precious manuscripts of the Scriptures. . . . From their mother's knee the Waldensian youth had been trained with this purpose in view; they understood their work and faithfully performed it (ibid., 67, 70).

Sacred ground drenched in blood

What did it cost the Waldensians to stand tall as families in an age when 99.9 percent of the people simply fell in line with a corrupt church and did as they were told? We followed the mountain road that wound its way above Torre Pellici. We parked our car and then continued on foot, over a trail followed by hundreds of Waldensians while their homes were being destroyed in the valley below. Following the signs, we arrived at last at a cave hidden in the forest. Immense slabs of rock thrown together by convulsing nature had formed this retreat. At first it seemed to us the cave went nowhere beyond the entrance. We had no flashlight but were able to use our camera flash to peer beyond. There was a huge underground room stretching to the left. Here they pressed their way, fathers and mothers carrying their aged and their infants to a place of safety. But their hiding place was betrayed, and their enemies built a large bonfire at the entrance to the cavern. Within its recesses, approximately three hundred had slowly suffocated.

We stood together on this sacred ground, consecrated by the blood of martyrs who wanted to live as we want to live today. They had dreams. They wanted to raise their infants and see their youth live to proclaim the truth to the dark regions beyond. Was the author of Hebrews thinking of such as these when he wrote:

> They wandered about in sheepskins and goatskins, being destitute, afflicted, tormented—of whom the world was not worthy. They wandered in deserts and mountains, in dens and caves of the earth (Heb. 11:37, 38, NKJV)?

The great English poet John Milton in 1655 wrote, "On the Late Massacre in Piedmont."[3] He says, in part:

> Avenge O Lord thy slaughtered Saints, whose bones
> Lie scatter'd on the Alpine mountains cold,
> Ev'n them who kept thy truth so pure of old
> When all our Fathers worship't Stocks and Stones.

Milton goes on to mourn the mother and infant being hurled down the rocky cliffs. The art of the time pictures bodies being dismembered and children being dashed against the rocks. The great poet finishes with a plea to flee out of Babylon.

Our day

What was the spirit that buoyed up the spirit of Waldensian families in their bloodstained path? "They believed that the end of all things was not far distant" (*The Great Controversy*, 72). The love of Jesus, the plan of salvation, and the hope of His soon appearing were truths they would share with others, even at the cost of life itself.

History will be repeated—this time on a worldwide scale. Many will be martyred before the close of probation, but the "blood of martyrs is the seed of the church." After the close of probation, Satan will influence governments all over the planet to proclaim a death decree for those who refuse to honor Sunday above the Sabbath of the fourth commandment. It would please the enemy to kill every faithful child of the King. But martyrdom would serve no purpose, since the case of every soul has already been decided. God will intervene and deliver His people. What a glorious day! We will have followed along the bloodstained path others have walked before. And now our families will be going home!

For your family

1. In what areas are we having difficulty holding fast to high standards?

_____ Are we sensitive about being ridiculed by the world?

_____ Does the culture encourage us to sin?

_____ Is it Satan's deceptions?

2. Dedicate one or more family worships to what history tells us about persecution. Prepare a family prayer that God

will help you be faithful, no matter what the cost. Record your prayer.

3. In what places of the world today are people being persecuted for standing for what is right? Discuss these as a family. What must it be like?

4. How can we teach our children to be strong for God in future persecution without causing them undue fear and anxiety? What has our family or group learned from the Waldensian story?

1.The term *barba* means "uncle," but the word was used in its feminine form. "The Waldensians used this term to refer to their pastors, perhaps in deliberate contrast with the Catholic practice of calling priests 'father' (Bouchard, Giorgio, *Christian History* VIII, no. 2, 12).

2 Tourn, Georgio, *You Are My Witnesses—The Waldensians Across 800 Years.* Torino, Italy: Claudiana Editrice, 1989, 41.

3 *Christian History* VIII, no. 2, 27.

CHAPTER

16

COMING OUT OF BABYLON——
Psychological Roadblocks

(John) In the fifteenth century, hundreds of splendid sailing vessels took their captains to distant lands and brought back to Europe samples of the exotic world of the East. But whether they were going around the Cape of Good Hope or the tip of India, mariners had one thing in common. As far as possible, they liked to keep land in sight, or if they couldn't, they liked to have a pretty good idea of the distance to and direction of land. The accepted geography of the day assumed a flat earth. Nobody wanted to venture too far into the unknown and fall off the deep end!

Actually, there were no physical barriers the technology of the time could not have bridged that would have impeded mariners in crossing to the new world. The compass had been invented centuries before. The barriers that existed were psychological. Columbus had faith. He even wrote his *Libro de las Profecías* (*Book of Prophecies*), in which he interpreted the prophecies of the Bible. He had a different perspective. In his mind, he pictured a round earth. On this round ball, he would sail to the fabled lands of the East and bring spices back by going west.

We read the prophecies of Revelation and find that

Coming Out of Babylon—Psychological Roadblocks

Babylon the Great, an evil spiritual entity symbolized by the literal city of ancient Babylon, is fallen. Its fall is almost complete. God's remnant are admonished in the strongest terms to flee from Babylon to safety. While there are organizational dimensions of Babylon that we will deal with briefly elsewhere, perhaps more important is the experiential dimension. No matter where our family lives, city or country, or whatever church claims our membership, in our hearts we may be living in the experience of Babylon. We seem loathe to leave this Babylonian experience. There are various reasons. Among these we will look at the spiritual dimension, the social dimension, and the material dimension. But first of all, let's examine the psychological roadblocks that impede our flight from the Babylonian experience.

"Group think"

On December 6, 1941, the high command for the Pacific, including U.S. Admiral Husband E. Kimmel, met and discussed the danger of war with Japan. There was group consensus that the Japanese would not attack. No movement of the Japanese fleet had been detected. Seas to the northwest were considered too rough to navigate in December, and to the south and west, nothing had been spotted. But Admiral Chuichi Nagumo had moved across the Pacific with a thirty-three-ship strike force under radio blackout, and the unnavigable northern route had been traversed. The true problem was not the barrier of the Pacific, it was the mindset of the American commanders who agreed that this could not be done. At 7:50 a.m. on Sunday morning, December 7, 183 Japanese planes descended on Pearl Harbor and nearby military installations. They were followed by a second wave of 168 aircraft. Within a few short hours, the ships on Battleship Row had been destroyed or seriously damaged, 347 aircraft were demolished, and more than 2,300 American military personnel were dead. The fact that "group think" had agreed the attack would not come did not deter the tragic reality.

In April of 1961, President John F. Kennedy's closest advisors met and finished a covert plan for the invasion of Cuba. In the course of a few days, a sort of mass psychology took over. Everybody seemed to be in favor. One experienced diplomat foresaw the international implications and approached Robert Kennedy, the Attorney General and brother and confidant of the president, and warned him before the final planning session that the negative factors and danger of failure of the operation had not been sufficiently weighed. Robert Kennedy dismissed the suggestion and stated that the president had already made up his mind to invade and that now what was needed was the support of everyone. The seasoned diplomat said no more. A few days later, on April 17, 1961, a force of fifteen hundred Cuban exiles landed at the Bay of Pigs. Diplomatic humiliation at the United Nations followed and within a few days, eleven hundred of the invaders were prisoners, in one of the worst fiascos of the cold war.

"Group think" is when the best judgment of individuals is paralyzed because they permit themselves to be carried along on the tide of majority opinion. This was illustrated in the destruction of Pompeii. We visited Pompeii and saw where, on August 24, A.D. 79, the great volcano Mt. Vesuvius had erupted. Some who abandoned their belongings and left immediately escaped, but many families stayed. A cloud of poisonous gas descended on the resort city. Then came a hail of eight to ten feet of pumice stones up to three inches in diameter, followed by a torrent of seven feet of white ash, which fell like snow on the doomed city. The fact that thousands felt it could never happen did not avert the tragedy that destroyed the city and every family who stayed behind.

Negative self-talk

The twelve spies had returned from their forty-day reconnaissance of the Promised Land. Ten of them reported that an invasion would be a military catastrophe. Phrases such as "we are not able to go up against the people, for they are stronger than we!" and "there we saw the giants, and we were like grasshoppers in our own sight!" were freely tossed around. But Caleb and Joshua gave a minority report. They said, "Let us go up at once and take possession, for we are well able to overcome it." Notice that the ten spies said, "we are not able," but Caleb and Joshua said, "we are well able."

Unfortunately, the congregation accepted the majority report. They wept all night and cried, "If only we had died in this wilderness!" In life, it is an axiom that "what you say is what you get." God heard their prayer, and the next day He told Moses to inform the people that "just as you have spoken in My hearing, so I will do to you." They prayed that they would die in the wilderness, and over the next thirty-eight years, that is exactly what happened.

Negative self-talk. It has a powerful influence on us. When we hear ourselves say something, we tend to believe what we hear. If we say that going home is impossible, our own words will paralyze us, and going home will be impossible. However, if, based on the promises of God, we use positive self-talk, God will say, "According to your faith be it unto you."

What would be the power of these words if we repeated them often in the family circle?

"By God's grace, we are going through together as a family to the heavenly kingdom!"

"This world is not our home!"

"We will be among the white-robed throng who have come out of Babylon, and we will march victoriously into the New Jerusalem!"

What you say is what you get.

Look with us a few years later. Joshua and Caleb are the only adults who left Egypt who have entered the Promised Land. The major conquests are over, and the inheritance is being distributed. The eighty-five-year-old Caleb comes forward to Joshua with a special request. He says, "I'm as strong today as when Moses sent us out forty-five years ago to spy out the land. But I have one favor to ask. You know where those giants live. The big ones. The sons of Anak. They are still up there in their walled city on top of the mountain in Hebron. I want this one last challenge for me and my family. That's the land I want to give my family as an inheritance forever. Give me this mountain!" He invades the impregnable fortress—he kills the awesome giants. Caleb rejoices that what God said would come to pass forty-five long years earlier has been fulfilled to the letter. What you say is what you get!

A few more years, and Joshua is old. He makes his farewell address. He proclaims, "One man of you shall chase a thousand, for the Lord your God is He who fights for you, as He has promised you" (Josh. 23:10). He reviews the greatness of God in bringing their fathers out of Egypt and in intervening to give them a home—the Promised Land. Then he says, "Choose for yourselves this day whom you will serve." Two options are, worshiping the gods Abraham left behind with his ancestors on the other side of the Euphrates, or worshiping the gods of the Canaanites in whose land they dwell. Then Joshua rises to the heights of eloquence as he stands before all Israel with his wife, children, and grandchildren. With a sweep of his hand, he includes his family as he resolutely says: "But as for me and my house, we will serve the Lord." His family will not return to Babylon nor will they as a corporate group have Babylon in their hearts. "We will serve the Lord!" What power was such positive affirmation in the life and inheritance of his loved ones!

Our personal family experience

Like thousands of other Christian families, we continually labor and intercede in our prayers for the eternal salvation of our children and grandchildren. One day, I was reviewing with our son Wes, now a missionary in Guam, how God had blessed him over the years. I mentioned that although we had intense struggles with the enemy during his and his brother John's formative years, I had always had the inner faith that God would save them for the kingdom. Reflectively, Wes responded, "That's exactly why we have followed the Lord!" Yes, what you say is what you get!

This book is being written at our mountain cabin in North Carolina. Here we are free from distractions. The nesting phoebe and her little ones, the indigo bunting, the pileated woodpecker, the scarlet tanager, the squirrels, the friendly rabbit, and the angels are our only companions. We have been accumulating odds and ends about the family and last-day events for much of our lives, and we have intended to write this book for years, but now under pressure of deadlines for Family Life International and the Pacific Press, we are turning out a first chapter-draft a day and finally three chapters a day of revised copy. It seemed impossible to accomplish. But we have learned that God takes our resolute desire and brings fulfillment.

Our mountain cabin brings to our memories countless promises God has brought to pass here over the last seventeen years. Our son, John, was taking a class in his construction engineering degree at Andrews University. The professor was explaining how building a second home in the country was beyond the economic possibilities of middle-income Americans. "Maybe that's what conventional wisdom says," John answered, "but our family has done it!" What we are saying is that God sees the soul's resolve, and if it is to His honor and glory, He brings it to pass.

We wanted the mountain cabin as a legacy for our children, a family project that all would work on and from which all would benefit. We wanted to have a peaceful place where we could write books and articles that could bless others, and we wanted a place in the country, because this is what God has instructed us to do. We praise His name that after fifteen years of pounding nails during our vacations, the Lord has given us this place. He has used our humble instrumentality to reach souls in this relatively unevangelized area, to bring others to the message. We said we wanted it to honor the Lord. We claimed God's promises. What you say is what you get!

My family has a history of electrical problems of the heart. My brother—just three years older than I—died ten years ago a few days after having received a pacemaker. Another brother has a pacemaker. In a recent summer in Moscow as I gave a family evangelism series, my extremities were cold during the whole trip. It was a blessed time, yet a time of continual prayer and stress. Upon returning to the States, I went in for my annual physical. As she took the electrocardiogram, the nurse looked at me quizzically and asked, "Do you feel all right?" She adjusted her controls and tried again. The circuitry between the upper and the lower chambers of the heart had closed down, and the ventricles were creating their own contractions at a rate of thirty-some beats a minute—and sometimes dipping into the twenties.

After pacemaker surgery, I was determined not to over-exert as my deceased brother had. For some months, I really over-protected myself. Many times daily, our prayers and the intercession of others went before the throne of grace for my health. I came progressively to the realization that I must venture out more by faith, and without being foolhardy, return to more physical activity and even exertion. I believe God is healing me, and I thank Him that we have never been more able to render spiritual and intellectual service than at the present moment. Believing in God's ongoing grace, I am pursuing my hobby of climbing the highest mountains of each state. This last weekend I added number fifteen to the list, hiking the eight miles round trip to climb Mt. Rogers, the highest mountain in Virginia. It was my second try on this mountain, the last time having been aborted after getting lost in the darkness with only a waning pocket flashlight about two miles from the summit. Again, our achievements for the Lord and for our own wellness will depend on what we believe, resolve, and say. What we say is what we get!

Jabez

Few stories in the Bible illustrate the overcoming of psychological barriers in order to attain spiritual excellence more than the history of Jabez. Tucked away among the "begats" in the Chronicles are two verses Inspiration has dedicated to this hero. (I have asked lots of people who Jabez was, and I can count on the fingers of one hand those who could respond accurately!)

> Now Jabez was more honorable than his brothers, and his mother called his name Jabez [which the margin interprets as meaning "He will cause pain"], saying, "because I bore him in pain." And Jabez called on the God of Israel saying, "Oh, that You would bless me indeed, and enlarge my territory [the margin says 'border,'], that Your hand would be with me, and that You would keep me from evil, that I may not cause pain!" So God granted him what he requested (1 Chronicles 4:9, 10, NKJV).

A strange story. A mother in painful labor gives her son the name *Pain*. As he grew up and played with the other children, they would say, "Here comes Pain." "You're a Pain!" Some children would have borne the marks of psychological trauma for life. But as Jabez emerged into manhood, he took stock of the past and thought of the future. Could he rise above the negative connotations of his heredity and the environment that had dogged him as long as he could remember? He came to a moment of heartfelt decision and resolved that his future would not be determined by his past or by what others thought of him. And he called out to God and said, "I want to do something great for You. I don't want to be a pain. Lord, bless me! Enlarge my border and my vision. May Your hand be with me, and may You keep me from my natural tendencies and sin." How eloquent are the last seven words of the history: "So God granted him what he requested." What you say is what you get!

Coming out of Babylon

I saw another angel coming down from heaven, having great authority, and the earth was illuminated with his glory. And he cried mightily with a loud voice, saying, "Babylon the great is fallen, is fallen . . ." And I heard another voice from heaven saying, "Come out of her, my people, lest you share in her sins, and lest you receive of her plagues" (Revelation 18:1, 2, 4, NKJV).

What are the psychological barriers that are keeping us as families from leaving Babylon?

For the millions in religious Babylon, perhaps timing is important. World crisis has not yet brought multitudes to the crucial deciding point. But why are so many in the church living a life more of the world than of Christ? May we hazard a few opinions:

1. Many Christians don't take the call to come out of Babylon seriously, on an experiential level. We are gliding downhill in neutral. Most everybody else is doing the same. We can't all be wrong! Maybe we can call this an inertia mindset.

2. The "It can't happen to us" syndrome. I am absorbed in a busy world, and I have plans to do this and the other before the end comes. My personal projections haven't included a full-blown, life-and-death crisis that would affect our family in the early future. But may we ask:

Did the projections of the U.S. military commanders of the Pacific keep the tragedy of Pearl Harbor from happening? Did the lingering hope of the inhabitants of Pompeii, that everything would work out all right, rescue their families from the volcanic eruption?

3. *We don't want to be precipitous in preparing for a crisis that doesn't happen as soon as we anticipated.* We don't want to look silly by being too early. Someone said to me, "This is the first generation of Seventh-day Adventists who don't believe Christ's coming is imminent and that He will come in their generation." Do you agree or disagree with this statement?

4. *As human beings, we naturally shrink from the unknown.* Since the fall of Babylon is associated with cataclysmic events and the disruption of civilization as we know it, our minds feel more at ease not dealing with this as an imminent reality. But the events surrounding the fall of Babylon and coming out of her don't need to be unknown to us. Although mysterious to the world, they are clearly revealed in Scripture.

5. *Could it be that some in heart actually see themselves as belonging in Babylon?* The children of Israel had been taken into Babylonian captivity. They had the writings of the prophet Jeremiah warning them to leave Babylon. Through Daniel's intervention before Cyrus, the way was providentially opened for their return. Three times, the decrees went forth encouraging them to return. However, relatively few chose to leave their comfortable Babylonian situation where many of them had become bankers and commercial traders. Yet there were a chosen few of whom Jeremiah could write:

"[They] seek the Lord their God. They shall ask the way to Zion, with their faces toward it" (Jeremiah 50:4, 5, NKJV).

9—U.C.

Friend, may your face and the faces of your family members be set toward Zion and away from Babylon. May you overcome every psychological roadblock as your family moves out of the Babylonian experience and into the covenant of hope.

For your family
1. What is Babylon?

Children's definition: Babylon is anything that takes us away from God. What might that be in our lives?

Adult definition: Do we know what our Babylon is? What is it that is causing "confusion" in our spiritual priorities and that is gluing us to earth, when God is calling us to "come out" into the freedom of His best plan for our lives? What is it that makes us more a citizen of the world than a citizen of heaven?

2. How about dancing, movies, and questionable TV programs? Some people argue and say, "What's wrong about that?" How would you feel about an approach of asking, "Is this God's best for me?"

When you participate in these activities, how do you feel about that powerful relationship with God in your spiritual life?

How would you answer someone who said, "Watching violence and romance on TV really doesn't affect me"?

Is reading the Bible and praying your delight? Can you pray, "Dear Jesus, I love You more than these"?

Someone said, "If anything destroys or interferes with our love for Jesus, then it is unsafe." Would you agree?

3. In what ways can we deliberately let go of earthly Babylonian magnets and be free to follow God's path home as a family?

What is keeping us back in Babylon as a family?

4. What if all members of the family are not willing to give up the comforts and pleasures of Babylon? What do we do?

Coming Out of Babylon—Psychological Roadblocks

Here is one suggested prayer:

Lord, open our eyes to the psychological and spiritual roadblocks that keep us from journeying toward the celestial city. Set us free from Babylon's bondage so our whole family can glorify God and go home to the earth made new. In Jesus' liberating name, Amen.

CHAPTER

17

COMING OUT OF BABYLON—
Material Roadblocks

The problem with getting to heaven is not geographical or logistical. It is not a question of how can we get a family from way down here to way up there. Our problem is not how to get families into heaven but how to get heaven into families! When heaven gets into the hearts of family members, the space question will take care of itself.

By the same token, our major problem is not getting families out of Babylon—the problem is getting Babylon out of families. Both Joseph and Daniel were carried against their wishes into captivity. However, when it came to principle, Joseph refused to live like the Egyptians, and Daniel chose not to live like the Babylonians. What Joseph was to Egypt and what Daniel was to Babylon, Seventh-day Adventist Christian families are to be to the world in which we live today.

One of the most basic differences between those who choose to leave Babylon and those who choose to stay in Babylon will be their philosophy on *things*, which is built on the basic reason they believe they're here on earth.

Coming Out of Babylon—Material Roadblocks

Founding principles of Babylon

The Bible tells us that soon after the Flood, Nimrod "began to be a mighty one on the earth" (Gen. 10:8, NKJV). He built a city called Babel. Within a few years, his descendants decided to build a tower that would reach to heaven. This was to glorify and make a name for themselves (Gen. 11:4)—to show their independence from God. God wanted them to scatter over the unpopulated earth, but they decided to settle in and do their own thing. God said "spread out," but they said "settle in." God had said there would never be another worldwide flood, but they didn't trust God's plan or His promise.

Centuries went by. Nebuchadnezzar became king of Babylon. Satan inspired him to build Babylon as the height of human achievement and the epitome of seductive error. Babylon was Satan's counterfeit for the New Jerusalem. As the king surveyed his handiwork, he bragged, "Is not this great Babylon, that I have built for a royal dwelling by my mighty power and for the honor of my majesty?" (Dan. 4:30, NKJV). Babylon was Satan's master plan. It was the materialization of a spiritual attitude against God.

God's master plan

God's master plan is just the opposite of Babylon's. The spiritual attitude of God's plan could not be more different. It is based on three eternal principles: (1) God is the owner of everything; (2) men and women are stewards; and (3) we are pilgrims on this earth, heading from Babylon toward the New Jerusalem. Let's briefly examine these three principles.

First, *God is the owner of everything*. The psalmist wrote: "The earth is the Lord's, and everything in it, the world, and all who live in it" (Psa. 24:1, NIV). Another prophet of antiquity acknowledged: " 'The silver is mine and the gold is mine,' declares the Lord Almighty" (Hag. 2:8, NIV). If we and all our assets belong to God, it follows that we must put Him *first* in our plans. This can take a lot of stress out of living, because when we follow His guidance, He makes Himself responsible for the results. When we recognize God's ownership and enter into this trusting son- and daughter-type relationship with Him, then He acknowledges that all His treasures belong to us. We become co-heirs with Christ to all the riches of the universe.

Second, *we are God's stewards*. God has entrusted money and wealth to us that we may carefully and thoughtfully manage them in His service. If He has given us a surplus above our basic needs, He is entrusting us with possessions to see if we will be faithful trustees helping to advance His work and bless others.

Third, *we are pilgrims on earth heading toward a better land*. Abraham lived in one of the most culturally advanced cities of the country, which would become Babylon. Yet he chose eternal riches, a city "which has foundations, whose builder and maker is God" (Heb. 11:10, NKJV). Moses esteemed "the reproach of Christ greater riches than the treasures in Egypt" (Heb. 11:26, NKJV).

John Stott, a prominent contemporary theologian, says:

> Contentment is the secret of inward peace. It remembers the stark truth that we brought nothing into the world and we can take nothing out of it. Life, in fact, is a pilgrimage from one moment of nakedness to another. So we should travel light and live simply. Our enemy is not possessions, but excess. Our battle cry is not "Nothing!" but "Enough!" We've got enough. Simplicity says, if we have food and clothing, we will be content with that (*Discipleship Journal*, 1989, 53:30).

David Augsburger comments:

> It's high time for Christians to choose to travel light. . . . It is time to sort out our values and to pare those we keep

down to the core, and to put the long-term eternal values in first place (Jack and Carole Maghall, "The Cash Clash," *Discipleship Journal*, 53:37).

At the gospel train station on earth, God calls: "Destination New Jerusalem! All aboard!" But another conductor calls: "Destination Babylon the Great! Enjoy! You're already here!"

Biblical heroes called out of materialism

The Bible tells the story of key individuals who turned their backs on what the earth could offer in order to journey heavenward. Moses could have had the treasures of Egypt (Heb. 11:26) and been buried in a magnificent tomb in the Valley of the Kings. But he heard God's call to lead His people out of Egyptian bondage, and he chose to suffer affliction with the people of God rather than to enjoy the pleasures of sin for a season. Today as you read these lines, Moses is in heaven—enjoying eternal riches.

Nicodemus had been fabulously rich. After Jesus' death, he came out openly and used his considerable wealth to support the struggling infant church in Jerusalem. He gave generously and eventually became poor by the world's standards. But he deemed no sacrifice too great to be able to serve Him who for our sakes became poor.

On the other hand, the rich young ruler came running to Jesus, anxious to be a follower of Christ. The Master saw that his idol was his riches and told him to give all he had to the poor and follow Him. The Bible says that Jesus looked at the young man and "loved him." Christ saw tremendous potential in this young member of the Sanhedrin. He could have authored books of the Bible. He could have been a follower, like Peter or John. He could have extended the triumphs of the gospel to lands afar. But he was not willing to heed the call out of materialism. He went away sorrowful, because he had many possessions.

Others called from materialism to sacrifice

About the year A.D. 1170, a wealthy merchant in Lyons, France, by the name of Waldo made some important personal decisions concerning his possessions. First, he commissioned the translation of several books of the Bible from Latin into the vernacular. Next, he abandoned his business and distributed his goods. He read Mark 10:22, that if you wish to be perfect, sell what you have and follow me, and he took it literally. We might argue today that this decision was radical, but this is beside the point. Waldo believed God had called him to leave all material possessions. This he did, and he dedicated his life as a layman to preaching the gospel message in public. Today the Waldensians claim him as their founder. He led thousands out of spiritual Babylon. His followers chose the blood-drenched path of sacrifice rather than the accepted culture of compromise.

John N. Andrews was only seventeen when his parents accepted the Sabbath truth in 1845. Brilliant and intellectually inclined, he had decided to study law. His uncle Charles was in politics and later became a member of Congress. When James and Ellen White visited John's hometown of Paris, Maine, in 1849, young Andrews witnessed the meeting where "the power of God came down upon the assembly, prostrating some. Parents confessed to their children, and children to their parents. John Andrews exclaimed, 'I would exchange a thousand errors for one truth' " (Spalding, *Origin and History of Seventh-day Adventists*, 1:208). In the *Review and Herald* of February 20, 1855, James White wrote, "Relatives have offered to give him a collegiate education free, or place him in a situation to acquire wealth; but these he refused, to follow in the despised path of Bible truth."

John Andrews traveled summer and winter in conditions that often compromised his health. His attitude was to brave tribulation with joy in his heart that "the work" might go forward. He said, "My heart is bound up in it, and in a work so sacred I would cheerfully spend and be spent" (Everett Dick, *Founders of the Message*, 303). The Andrews family, with young John broken in health, moved west in the autumn of 1855 and settled near Waukon, Iowa. In December of the following year, James and Ellen White braved winter snows and traveled by sleigh for many days from Illinois toward Waukon. When they reached the Mississippi River, they crossed by faith, even though the ice was thin and covered by almost a foot of water. They held meetings in Waukon, which resulted in the reclaiming of a discouraged John Andrews (and his friend John Loughborough) for the ministry.

Andrews became the first officially sponsored SDA overseas missionary and sailed from Boston in 1874. He did "cheerfully spend and be spent." Andrews died of tuberculosis in Basel, Switzerland, in 1883, leaving a legacy of the thriving missionary journal *Les Signes des Temps* and a number of organized and growing churches in Switzerland, France, Germany, Italy, and Poland. His family had come out of popular religions and decided to keep the Sabbath when he was seventeen. At age twenty-one, young John turned his back on a possibly lucrative career in law to follow truth wherever it led. At age twenty-eight, he turned away from the fertile Iowa farmland for the uncertainties of preaching the last-day message. Three times God called him to come out and be separate. Andrews left materialism behind and journeyed with sacrifice toward a better land. Will he regret those choices in eternity?

Leave Babylonian materialism? Why?

Why do people like Babylon? Because of something in our fallen human nature, if given the choice between the material and the more ethereal, nine people out of ten will go for present enjoyment rather than future hope. Our Babylon is a comfortable place. It is convenient, highly cultured, and technologically advanced. It seems to be a good place in which to live. When Ezra, under the decree of Artaxerxes, called for the Jews to leave Babylon, relatively few elected to leave. The great majority decided to stay behind rather than to risk the *uncertainties* of starting a new life in Judea.

We may like the housing and personal lifestyle of our Babylon. It may include luxurious houses and extravagant apparel. People spend what they don't have to live in the fast lane and to indulge themselves. These things can impress our neighbors. Our adornments are status symbols so others will see how wonderful and stunning we are. Babylon is based on the "get" principle, and there are a lot of things to get.

But God knows these present things are just so many chains that will keep us from enjoying eternal riches and happiness. Real happiness is not found in getting but in giving. Why spend money we don't have to buy things we don't need to impress people we don't like? As the Bible says, "The borrower is servant [or slave] to the lender" (Prov. 22:7, NKJV). Indebtedness is a modern form of slavery, and God said in Exodus 20:2 that He has called us "*out* of the house of bondage" (NKJV, emphasis supplied).

Ellen White makes these two strong statements regarding debt:

"When one becomes involved in debt, he is in one of Satan's nets, which he sets for souls" (*The Adventist Home*, 392).

"Deny yourself a thousand things rather than run in debt. . . . Avoid it as you would the smallpox" (*The Adventist Home*, 393).

God doesn't want us caught in a net or in an epidemic. God wants us to be free from debt. Only then will we be able to go where He wants us to go and do what He wants us to do. How many people have you heard of whom God has called to some exciting and needy field, but they could not go— their financial bondage impeded them.

God wants to call us to eternal and worthwhile priorities

in life. He wants us to have priorities that won't go down the tube in a disaster. Christ wants us to have the abundant life.

He says: "I have come that they may have life, and that they may have it more abundantly" (John 10:10, NKJV). But to give us that abundance, He must cut away everything that might deprive us of it. To enter the New-Jerusalem experience, we must abandon the Babylonian experience.

Christ knows what will bring us true happiness. It is not *things*. On one occasion when dealing with a man who was in materialistic bondage, Christ said: "Take heed and beware of covetousness, for one's life does not consist in the abundance of the things he possesses" (Luke 12:15, NKJV). Christ doesn't want to see us disappointed in our investments. That's why He said: "Do not lay up for yourselves treasures on earth, where moth and rust destroy and where thieves break in and steal; but lay up for yourselves treasure in heaven, where neither moth nor rust destroys and where thieves do not break in and steal" (Matthew 6:19, 20, NKJV).

God knows that what we keep, we lose—and what we give, we keep. There is no joy like that of seeing the poor fed or the cold clothed. He gave us the example of Job, who searched out the needs of others. "The cause which I knew not, I searched out" (Job 29:16, KJV).

God sees that because of spreading wickedness, cities will soon become almost uninhabitable. He would rather see us leave the great population centers with time left, rather than just escaping by the skin of our teeth. If Lot would have come out of Sodom when Providence indicated, he would have still been able to use his possessions to God's honor and glory, and he would have saved his family. Because he turned a deaf ear to God's early call, Lot escaped only because the angels took him by the hand, "having mercy on him." All he took with him were the clothes on his back and his two daughters. The destruction of Sodom illustrates the destruction of the world. Ellen White says that she saw a great ball of fire fall among beautiful mansions. The people mourned, " 'We knew that the judgments of God were coming upon the earth, but we did not know that they would come so soon' " (*Testimonies for the Church*, 9:28).

Summary

Let's summarize, in outline form, the differences in viewpoint on the material things of life between Babylon and those who are called out to freedom:

The Babylonian Lifestyle vs. *The "Called Out" Experience*

1. What I have is mine	1. All I have belongs to God
2. I do what I want with my money	2. I am a steward to do what God wants
3. Excess	3. I have *enough* to meet necessities
4. Self-indulgence	4. Self-denial
5. Abuse	5. Use
6. Possessing is the *summum bonum* or "good life"	6. Pleasing God is the *summum bonum*
7. Getting	7. Giving
8. Hoarding	8. Saving
9. Worrying	9. Contentment
10. Live beyond my means	10. Live within my means
11. "She glorified herself" (Rev. 18:7)	11. Glorifying God
12. Luxury—"lived luxuriously" (Rev. 18:7)	12. Utility
13. Live for display— Rev. 18:11-13 Display of gold, apparel, jewels	13. Live for service
14. Live for the here and now	14. Live for eternity

Coming Out of Babylon—Material Roadblocks

Jesus counseled us: "Take heed to yourselves, lest your hearts be weighed down with carousing, drunkenness, and cares of this life, and that Day come on you unexpectedly. For it will come as a snare on all those who dwell on the face of the whole earth. Watch therefore, and pray always that you may be counted worthy to escape all these things that will come to pass, and to stand before the Son of Man" (Luke 21:34-36, NKJV).

Paul speaks of the attitude dedicated followers of Jesus should have in the last days. He says: "This I say, brethren, the time is short, so that from now on . . . those who buy [should be] as though they did not possess, and those who use this world as not misusing it. For the form of this world is passing away" (1 Corinthians 7:29-31, NKJV).

If we have Babylon in our hearts, if material things are more important than eternal, then when Babylon passes away, we will pass away with it. God doesn't want that to happen to us. He calls us to something better. His clarion call is "Babylon the great is fallen, is fallen. . . . Come out of her, my people, lest you share in her sins, and lest you receive of her plagues" (Rev. 18:2, 4, NKJV).

For your family

1. What are the basic material possessions that would make up "enough" for you today?

2. Someone has said that we spend the first half of our adult lives trying to get more things and the last half trying to get rid of them! How can you travel "light" as you journey toward the kingdom?

3. What can you do as a family to get out of financial bondage? What are you willing to give up in order to get out of debt?

4. At His death, Jesus gave His clothes to the soldiers, He entrusted His mother to John, and to the world He bequeathed the gospel of eternal life. When you die, what will

be your bequest?

5. Are there any material possessions hindering you from coming out of Babylon?

6. Have a garage sale and give half of the proceeds to the poor and half to spreading the gospel among unreached people groups.

CHAPTER

18

COMING OUT OF BABYLON—
Family Dynamics

(**Millie**) The influence of shared lives in the family is very great—husbands and wives, parents and children—each one, day by day, exercise a magnetism that draws those they love. This attraction may be toward loyalty to God, or it may be a pull toward Babylon and the world system.

God's startling message to come out of Babylon (a lifestyle that has no place for God on His terms) will find people and families in many different circumstances. Some families have been together in Babylon—and together they will decide to come out. Some who have been in Babylon will choose to leave, while others stay behind. In some cases, certain family members left Babylon years ago, and now, with the last invitation to those still there, will choose to stay behind or to join in the journey toward the kingdom.

God wants united families. Much can be said for the necessity of peace and harmony among relatives. What will happen when one feels called out of Babylon and a spouse or children do not accept the same call? Here, the words of Christ are and will be fulfilled:

"Do not think that I came to bring peace on earth. I did not come to bring peace but a sword. For I have come to 'set

143

a man against his father, a daughter against her mother, and a daughter-in-law against her mother-in-law.' And 'a man's foes will be those of his own household.' He who loves father or mother more than Me is not worthy of Me. And he who loves son or daughter more than Me is not worthy of Me" (Matthew 10:34-37, NKJV).

In the last few years, even as the world seems to be falling apart, the Lord and the unconditional love of family members are working miracles. We are witnessing many families leaving an empty Babylonian lifestyle and joining together in the journey to a better land. Here are a couple of these experiences.

Children coming out of Babylon

Mike was an adopted child who grew up in a Christian home where God's Word was reverenced. There was morning and evening worship. He attended Christian schools. As he came to the age when his classmates and some close cousins committed themselves to the Lord and were baptized, Mike drew back. He wasn't ready for a commitment to Jesus. Years of indecision stretched on through adolescence and into young adulthood. The invitation was given again and again, but there was no positive response. Eventually, he moved out from under his parents' protecting roof and launched himself into "the fast lane."

At length his parents accepted a call to the mission field, but morning and evening, from their family altar, incense of intercession arose in favor of their son, Mike. Mike's father regularly rose early to implore God for divine intervention in the conversion of their son. This went on for years. One morning his father was praying again, and his prayer went something like this: "Dear Lord, here I am again with my elbows leaning on the balcony of heaven praying for Mike. Lord, my elbows are getting tired, but I don't want to let go until this prayer is answered." A peace came over this agonizing father. It seemed as if God were telling him, "I love Mike even more than you do, and I've got some surprises coming up for you."

A few days later at work thousands of miles away, an idea formed in Mike's mind as to how he could pull off a shady deal and pocket a sum of money. Suddenly a voice spoke to him and said, "Mike, this is your *last* chance!" Mike was so startled that he looked around to see who had spoken, but he saw no one. Conviction settled on his heart by the work of the Holy Spirit. That week he accepted Jesus as his personal Saviour. Christ had won the battle for his soul. Mike sensed God's call to service, studied at the seminary, and today is a successful gospel minister. What rejoicing there was in two fathers' hearts—heavenly and earthly!

We had been praying for a certain family for several years. The parents and their grown children scarcely spoke to one another and had severed all social contact. The married daughter fell ill with cancer, her mother's words to her during a quarrel ringing in her ears: "I never want to see you again!" We tried to bridge the gulf. We failed.

One Sabbath afternoon after studying the prophecy of Malachi 4 with the mother, we knelt together in a circle and interceded with tears that God would turn the hearts of the estranged mother and daughter to each other. In faith, our little group claimed God's healing of relationships, even though there was no visible evidence of change.

Sunday morning the mother called us as early as she dared. With joy in her voice, she asked, "Do you know who phoned me last night? At 2:00 a.m., my telephone rang, and a timid voice on the other end of the line whispered, 'Mother, I love you!' It was our daughter Nelda!" They talked for more than an hour, abandoning their longstanding hostilities and forgiving each other. The two of us responded, "Praise the Lord!" and rejoiced with her. Was that call a coincidence?

We don't think so. We believe that God directly intervenes in answer to intercessory prayer.

Others have prayed for years for wayward children and still haven't seen definite results. One father told me that he and his wife have been praying earnestly for twenty-five years and still haven't seen their son converted. But he told me that God had been preciously close and had given him a dream in which he saw his son David on the platform of the old home church giving his testimony of how he had found the Lord. The father said, "That is the day that I am living for." We and others have joined with this couple in praying for their son, even as they also are praying for ours, who, although they have never overtly turned their backs on the Lord, still need continual prayer cover in the crises they face from day to day. No, there is no immovable guarantee that children will always return. God will not force them into heaven against their will. No, there is no pat explanation for the agonizing pain of losing a child who never embraced God. These three things we can do: love, risk the pain of not knowing the answers, and pray.

Children praying for parents

Recently a group of students in a Christian college joined in an all-night prayer vigil. Do you know what kind of prayers predominated? The leader told us she had thought the students would pray for themselves and their own needs, but their greatest concern, it turned out, was the spiritual condition of their parents. Intercessory prayer is not always parents praying for children, but—thank God—many children are also praying their parents through spiritual crises.

While teaching elementary school in Texas, I always invited the children to share their prayer requests. A brother and sister would frequently ask that we pray for their father, who did not know the Lord. After several years, one Sabbath evening in an evangelistic meeting, the pastor made a call.

Coming Out of Babylon—Family Dynamics

The choir sang—intercessory prayers ascended to heaven. The father hesitated but then rose to his feet and walked to the front. This answer to the prayers of a son and a daughter for their father moved the congregation to tears. Overcome with emotion, the choir stopped singing. Joy filled every heart, because another family had begun moving together toward the kingdom of heaven.

The following true story comes from my neighbors. Some fifty years ago, the wife's brother—a minister—lost his way on moral issues. He eventually divorced his wife and gave up the church. Over a period of five decades, he was defensive and wouldn't allow his children or siblings to speak to him about his soul. Our neighbors just came back from celebrating the brother's ninety-first birthday. The miracle: He is coming back to the church. Old and almost blind, his heart has turned. His present wife has had no church affiliation, but since her husband's eyesight is failing, she has read him the Bible and other books Adventists love so well. They have both requested baptism for next month. His grandson, who is a pastor, will officiate at the service. Will there not be joy both in heaven and on earth that the mistakes of one more lifetime have been put behind and one more soul has come home?

Nothing pleases God more than to have His Word quoted back to Him in prayer and to have His promises claimed on behalf of saving the lost. He delights as we storm the enemy's strongholds to rescue captives through prayer. Second Corinthians 10:4 says, "For the weapons of our warfare are not carnal but mighty in God for pulling down strongholds" (NKJV). Luke 11:21-23 says, "When a strong man [Satan], fully armed, guards his own palace [the world], his goods [humankind everywhere] are in peace. But when a stronger than he [Christ] comes upon him and overcomes him, he takes from him all his armor in which he trusted, and divides his spoils" (NKJV). God does not propose to force us into heaven against our will, but thanks to the prayers of the saints, He does liberate the captives from bondage so they can again make a free choice—for God or for Satan. Our prayers authorize God to cross Satan's boundaries and once again intervene in lives. By intercessory prayer, we can storm the gates of the enemy. The Lord can initiate a chain of events that ultimately will lead many (indeed, the vast majority) of those we perseveringly pray for back to Him. This is what it means to be a priest. It is the priesthood of all believers (Exod. 19:6; 1 Pet. 2:9)—fathers, mothers, children interceding for one another—praying one another over life's rough places and on toward the kingdom.

Biblical promises for family members in Babylon

One of our favorite Bible promises is Isaiah 52:7-12. We use it, combining various Bible versions. We will leave blanks for you to fill in the names that apply to your situation. The picture is that of a runner approaching Jerusalem, coming over the mountains bringing good tidings. It is applied here to children coming home from Babylon.

" 'They're coming home! Good news. Your God [not the enemy, but God] reigns in Zion.' The watchmen shout and sing with joy, for right before their eyes they see the Lord God bring _____ home again. The Lord has bared his holy arm before the eyes of _____; _____ shall see the salvation of our God. Go now, _____ _____, leave your bonds and slavery. Put Babylon and all it represents far behind you. The Lord will go before you, _____, and the God of Israel will be your rear guard."

Here is another promise (fill in the blanks):

"This is my covenant with _____, saith the Lord; My spirit . . . is upon _____, and my words which I have put in _____ mouth, shall not depart out of _____ mouth, nor out of the mouth of thy seed [_____], nor out of the mouth of thy seed's seed [_____], saith the Lord, from henceforth and forever" (Isa. 59:21, KJV).

We are told that "It is a part of God's plan to grant us, in answer to the prayer of faith, that which He would not bestow did we not thus ask" (*The Great Controversy*, 525). With the promises of God's Word and all these heavenly blessings available on our knees, isn't it strange that we pray so little? Well might the Almighty wonder: "He saw that there was no man, and wondered that there was no intercessor" (Isa. 59:16, KJV).

Jesus says, "I gave My life's blood to redeem your son, your daughter, your father, your mother, your friend. I can't understand why you aren't interceding for your own flesh and loved ones when I gave My all." God is waiting. Will *you* intercede before it is too late?

For your family

1. Consider three interesting quotations and their meaning. The book *The Great Controversy* has three interesting statements about the effect of the call out of Babylon on family members. In the near future—or perhaps even now—we will see various reactions of family members as the call out of Babylon is heard by those we love. May these three quotes raise questions and answers that will strengthen our intercessory experience. The first quotation refers to families in 1843–1844, when many were expecting Jesus to come. Thousands were disfellowshiped from the popular churches, and families had to make agonizing decisions.

> The hearts of parents were turned to their children, and the hearts of children to their parents. The barriers of pride and reserve were swept away. Heartfelt confessions were made, and the members of the household labored for the salvation of those who were

nearest and dearest. . . . Many wrestled all night in prayer . . . for the conversion of their relatives or neighbors (*The Great Controversy*, 369).

Discussion Questions:

A. In a time of crisis, does your family pull together or pull apart? What can you do to handle problems in a better way?

If parents or children were willing to confess wrongs they have done over the years, this would impact other family members' thinking about accepting the call out of Babylon. What would be involved in healthy, noncontrolling, heartfelt confession? What would happen?

As we approach the great final crisis when the Holy Spirit is poured out in latter-rain power to prepare people for the time of trouble, some families will try to control their family members at whatever cost.

Conscientious obedience to the word of God will be treated as rebellion. Blinded by Satan, the parent will exercise harshness and severity toward the believing child. . . . Affection will be alienated; children will be disinherited, and driven from home. The words of Paul will be literally fulfilled: "All that will live godly in Christ Jesus shall suffer persecution" (*The Great Controversy*, 608).

Now the rays of light penetrate everywhere, the truth is seen in its clearness, and the honest children of God sever the bands which have held them. Family connections, church relations, are powerless to stay them now. Truth is more precious than all besides. Notwithstanding the agencies combined against the truth, a large number take their stand upon the Lord's side (*The Great Controversy*, 612).

B. If a relative were to demand that you follow family custom or culture instead of following Bible truth, what would you do?

C. What can you do now to make it easier for your family to be together on God's side in the last final conflict?

2. Heart turning can take place when:

_____ The Holy Spirit works in families.

_____ Family members say, "I'm sorry. Forgive me." The words "I love you" are expressed frequently by fathers and mothers to their children and by children to their parents.

Past hurts, anger, and resentments are given and released to God.

3. What steps are being taken in your family for heart turning and healing relationships?

4. Promises to claim for family members:

If Christian parents seek Him earnestly, He will fill their mouths with arguments, and for His name's sake will work mightily in their behalf in the conversion of their children (*Testimonies for the Church*, 5:323).

Those who accept the one principle of making the service and honor of God supreme will find perplexities vanish, and a plain path before their feet (*The Desire of Ages*, 330).

CHAPTER
19

THE HOLY SPIRIT DRAWS US HOME

(John) Have you ever seen a rainbow spanning the heavens? The storm has been raging, but the sunshine breaks through. Sometimes we even see double rainbows, the second one being like a mirror image of the first, with the colors showing in the reverse order. The families that go through the last-day storm will let the sunshine break through. They will be characterized by a rainbow of beautiful traits. The trials and storms of the last days, in the sunshine of Christ's righteousness, will bring out all the panorama of the beautiful hues of Christ's character in us.

Just as there are seven colors in the rainbow, there are seven Spirits of God (Rev. 5:6) which, like lamps, are burning before the throne. The Spirit in His completeness contains every beautiful trait we will ever need. Isaiah 11:2-4 even names these traits—the Spirit of wisdom, understanding, the Spirit of counsel, might (power), the Spirit of knowledge, fear of the Lord, and judgment. And to think that, by God's grace, we can be filled with all the fullness of the Spirit! Sometimes in the morning, the two of us pray down through this list because we know we can't make it through the day without the Spirit's wisdom, counsel, or judgment. But when we accept the Holy Spirit, He brings *every* blessing in His train.

A pastor was finishing up a series of evangelistic meetings. It was Sabbath morning, and the advertised topic was "The Mark of the Beast." He, his church, and the whole conference had been praying for the outpouring of the Holy Spirit. However, it was with trepidation that the pastor viewed a group of forty visitors he had never seen before arriving shortly before his sermon. What to do? He wanted to change the sermon, but he just could not think of any other one to preach. He had no other notes with him, so he proceeded to preach on the Mark of the Beast.

After the sermon, three families, all related and representing the group of forty, came to the pastor. They told him that for a year they had been studying together in the Bible and said, "We found the Sabbath in our studies." The week before, someone had said, "Let us go to a Sabbath-keeping church instead of meeting by ourselves." They went to the telephone directory and found a strange name listed in the yellow pages—"Seventh-day Adventist Church"—with worship services on Saturday. In their study, they were convinced that the Sabbath was right and believed that the Sabbath had been changed, but they did not know who had changed it or why. After hearing the sermon, they said, "Now, we know." They asked the pastor, "Would it be possible for you to join our Bible-study group?" The Holy Spirit, in His tender kindness, was calling an extended family group to the blessings of new fellowship with God's remnant church and to preparing for the great homecoming when Jesus will soon take our families to heaven.

Have you ever worried whether or not you will ever make it through the difficult days ahead? Are you concerned your family might not have what it takes to make it to heaven without the loss of one? Good news! Although the Spirit is being withdrawn from the earth, even as it was in the days of

Noah, God is giving an extra portion of this same Spirit to all who ask for it humbly and in faith. He has already given us the Holy Spirit, which has sealed us as His and which constitutes the guarantee or down payment that He who has begun a good work in us will carry it through to completion to the praise of His glory (Ephesians 1:13, 14). He will supply your family's every spiritual need. He will see to it that the character of Jesus is reproduced in your family as together you claim the merits of His blood.

The last generation of the saved will be the most loving generation in history, growing up in the midst of a world that hates. They will be the most loyal, growing up in the midst of a world that is rebellious. They will be the most truthful, growing up in a world that believes and makes a lie. They will be the purest, living in a world corrupted by immorality. Where will the last-day family obtain these characteristics? Certainly, they are not self-generated. These are the attributes of the Holy Spirit, which have been brought into human lives as a gift and which will transform personalities as the Spirit applies what Christ already had done for us on Calvary.

What the Holy Spirit does for your family

One of the first blessings the Spirit will bring to your home will be a sweet atmosphere. The song written by Doris Akers in 1965 "A Sweet, Sweet Spirit in This Place" describes what we are looking for.

When I was a child, we would have morning and evening worship in our home. I was the smallest, and I didn't always understand what the older ones were reading or singing about. We often sang the song that said, "Peace, peace, sweet peace, Wonderful gift from above." I thought the song was about flowers, and I would sing, "Peas, peas, sweet peas, Wonderful gift from above." Maybe I was right in my song too. There is a fragrance—like the perfume of sweet peas—that comes from above. This wonderful gift—the sweet Holy Spirit—

brings to our homes a sweetness, a fragrance, a peace. Ellen White describes the Spirit-filled home:

> The sweetest type of heaven is a home where the Spirit of the Lord presides. If the will of God is fulfilled, the husband and wife will respect each other and cultivate love and confidence (*The Adventist Home*, 15).

Home—the sweetest type of heaven. A place where love is cultivated. Our problem is that we have been cultivating the brambles and thorns of discord when we should have been cultivating the "sweet peas" of the Spirit. The Holy Spirit is the only power that can bring harmony into our homes. This abiding peace will not only pervade our family but its influence will bring a freshness to our neighborhood and to the weary and burdened who may contact us.

> The Spirit of Christ will be an abiding influence in the home life. If men and women will open their hearts to the heavenly influence of truth and love, these principles will flow forth again like streams in the desert, refreshing all and causing freshness to appear where now is barrenness and dearth (*Child Guidance*, 484).

What does the Holy Spirit have to do with family unity? "The fruit of the Spirit is love, joy, peace, longsuffering, kindness, goodness, faithfulness, gentleness, self-control. . . . If we live in the Spirit, let us also walk in the Spirit" (Gal. 5:22, 23, 25, NKJV). It is the Holy Spirit who will give the family the relationships (vertical and horizontal) that will make them victorious in the last days.

A Christian pastor had been finishing his Doctor of Ministry degree and couldn't decide what he should write his dissertation on. Finally, he was convinced that he should choose the subject "Family—School of Love." For many months, he gathered materials on this topic. He noted that God is love and that the primary manifestation of the fruit of the Spirit is love. He made out a curriculum that he could use in the churches he might pastor, and even more important, he practiced, in his own home, all the things he was learning.

One evening for worship, this father asked all the family members to write a love note to all other members of the family saying what they liked about them. His little four-year-old daughter could not write, so Dad wrote down what she dictated for her brother, mother, and for himself. All the love notes were collected, and the three notes were delivered to each person. Then each individual read the love notes the other three members of the family had written. When the turn of the little girl came, again she had the problem that she could not read. So Dad read the notes to her as she self-consciously fingered her little dress. When Dad had finished, this little four-year-old threw her arms around his neck and said, "Daddy, I love you *so* much!" Here was a family that was making the greatest preparation for the difficult days ahead.

The families that won't make it are those characterized as "lovers of themselves, lovers of money, boasters, proud, blasphemers, disobedient to parents, unthankful, unholy, unloving, unforgiving, slanderers, without self-control, brutal, despisers of good" (2 Timothy 3:2, 3, NKJV). What's their problem? It is simply that they haven't submitted to the Holy Spirit, who was willing and anxious to give them love and sweet peace.

What will provide the necessary motivation that causes families to leave Babylon and head toward the heavenly home? Will it be intellectual arguments? Hardly. There are intellectual reasons to stay in Babylon that make good sense to a lot of people. Will it be the desire for the inestimable wealth and riches of heaven? Riches "some day in heaven" wouldn't be sufficient motivation to cause people to turn their backs on riches here, and certainly not motivation to suffer persecution and the threat of death if they obey all the commandments of God.

We've concluded that the Holy Spirit is the only motivating force strong enough to enable families to make this life-and-death decision. The Holy Spirit does not force us out of Babylon and sin. It presents us with the alternatives and captures our hearts with Christ's love. True, there are material riches that await us in heaven. There is the Holy City, the New Jerusalem, which awaits the conqueror. Christ gives us the most powerful reasons to head toward the heavenly home. But ultimately, the great motivators will appeal to our spiritual nature. The greatest one will be to be with Jesus, who has died to redeem us—to spend eternity with Him. The Spirit pleads, convinces, and draws. In the last chapter of the Bible is the final invitation mentioned in Scripture: "The Spirit and the bride say, 'Come!' And let him who hears say, 'Come!' And let him who thirsts come. And whoever desires, let him take the water of life freely" (Revelation 22:17, NKJV).

The story of a Spirit-led revival

A few years ago, we made the effort and visited Herrnhut, then in East Germany. We wanted to know more about the Moravians and about Count Zinzendorf of Saxony, who led this unusual settlement. Refugees from assorted Christian beliefs made their way there. They included United Brethren, Pietists, Anabaptists, Roman Catholics, and Lutherans (Zinzendorf himself was a Lutheran). Their variety brought much discord into the community. On May 12, 1727, Zinzendorf called the settlers together and addressed them on the evils of separation and the blessedness of Christian unity. They then signed a "Brotherly Agreement": forty-two Statutes to move them toward Christian fellowship. "The events on May 12 initiated a month's long period of religious revival in which previous discords were dissolved, so that Herrnhut, during the summer of 1727, became a brotherhood" (Weinlick, *Count Zinzendorf*, 76).

The climax came at the Wednesday morning Communion service on August 13, 1727. The Holy Spirit descended upon the people with such power they hardly knew whether they were in heaven or on earth. The effect was so strong that members of their community working twenty miles away and unaware the meeting was taking place were deeply conscious of the Spirit filling their lives.

So it was that in 1727 commenced an around-the-clock "prayer watch" that continued nonstop for over a hundred years (Tarr, *Christian History*, vol. 1, no. 1, 18). When we were there, we inquired from our Moravian guide if this was true, and she told us that indeed the around-the-clock vigil still continues today, over 250 years later, but now it includes various Moravian communities that take part around the world. Moravians celebrate August 13 as the birthday of their Spirit-filled movement.

What were the results? In twenty years, the Moravians sent out more missionaries than all other Protestant groups had sent in two hundred years (*Christian History*, vol. 1, no. 1, 6). Note well that we don't receive the Holy Spirit for personal edification or self-actualization. We receive the heavenly gift to enable us to witness to others of the power of Jesus Christ to change our life and our family. Our family is part of the earthly family, soon to be reunited with the heavenly family. Our greatest resource in preparation and in witnessing to others so they can prepare is active partnership with the Holy Spirit in our home.

Is your home a little heaven on earth—a little heaven to go to heaven in?

The Holy Spirit Draws Us Home

For your family

1. Have you ever been to a meeting, or have you ever had an experience in your personal life, when you felt the unmistakable presence of the Holy Spirit? If so, tell the story to your family.

2. What steps could you take as a family to have more harmony and a "sweet spirit" that would make the heavenly gift feel welcome in your home? Are there any hard feelings between family members? Are there unconfessed sins that separate members of your family?

CHAPTER
20

CHILDREN GOING HOME

"We need not fear that our children
will stand tall before man
if they have bowed low before God."

(John and Millie) Little Sulvig was only 8 and her sister Christa was 6. As the people gathered in the meetinghouse, Sulvig and Christa could see small groups huddling in the corners. Cautiously, Sulvig sneaked a little closer and strained her ears to hear what the big people were whispering about. "Brother Olafson was thrown into jail today," one uncle said, "and the town officials say that any man or woman who publicly preaches, against the teachings of the state church, that Jesus is coming soon will be immediately imprisoned!"

It was time for the meeting to begin. As the people took their seats, a policeman entered and sat in the last pew. Sulvig noted glances passing between her daddy—who was the deacon—and the elder of the church. No one moved. It was so quiet she thought she could hear her own heart pounding. She could see her mother's lips moving, though her eyes were closed—*she must be praying*, Sulvig thought. After a bit, someone began to sing. Everyone joined in, but no one dared to speak.

Suddenly Sulvig found herself walking to the platform. Who was that by her side? It was Christa. Sulvig began to speak—not that she wanted to. Somehow it seemed as if Jesus and the angels were speaking through her. She wasn't afraid. The people craned their necks trying to see her, but Daddy came to the rescue and set her and Christa on top of the table. All the Bible texts she had learned seemed to just roll out—the very same promises she had heard in family worship. Without fear, she told the people that Jesus was coming soon. Her sister, who couldn't even read yet, spoke out against drinking alcohol. Sulvig watched as the town drunk fell to his knees, pleading, "God, be merciful to me, a sinner." Others also began to call to God for mercy, and a Mr. Johnson, who had stolen something from her daddy years before, crossed the aisle and with tears in his eyes said he was sorry. Everybody looked happy now, except the policeman, who had turned decidedly pale. Suddenly he got up and left. Sulvig felt good that even though the big people couldn't say anything, God had spoken through her and had shared the good news that Jesus was coming soon (John and Millie Youngberg, Adapted from *Rebuilding the Family Altar*, 67, 68).

History records that when the law prohibited men and women from preaching in Scandinavia during the 1840s, the Holy Spirit came upon young children, who then proclaimed the message. Will this ever happen again? Ellen White tells us:

In the closing scenes of this earth's history many of these children and youth will astonish people by their witness to the truth, which will be borne in simplicity, yet with spirit and power. They have been taught the fear of the Lord, and their hearts have been softened by a careful and prayerful study of the Bible. In the near future many children will be endued with the Spirit of God, and will do a work in proclaiming the truth to the world, that at that time cannot well be done by the older members of the church *(Counsels to Parents and Teachers*, 166, 167).

It grips our hearts to think of the miracle of our children preaching the message during the latter rain. But miracles are already happening as angels speak through children in our days. Garrie Williams, in his book *Welcome, Holy Spirit,* reports an incident in Brazil during one of his meetings: an eight- or nine-year-old girl prayed for those present at the meeting and especially for her unconverted father. God's Spirit touched the heart of this father, and when the call was made, he came forward and surrendered his life fully to Jesus Christ.

Isn't it beautiful that when the Holy Spirit works, even little children have a burden for the conversion of their unsaved parents? As parents, we need also to have a burden to see our children grow and become "strong in spirit" like John the Baptist. What can we do to cooperate with the powerful divine agencies that are already working in our children's hearts? Undoubtedly we could make a long list, but let's limit ourselves to five things:

1. Share yourself with your children and grandchildren.
2. Rediscover with them the excitement, wonder, and magic of the child's world. Enjoy!
3. Tell the great stories—the great narratives.

4. Nurture the positives while pruning the negatives.

5. Pray with and for your children.

What parents can do

1. Share yourself with your children and grandchildren. There is no greater favor you can do for children. We want them to be trained for service. How do we do it? By serving others ourselves and inviting them to join in the fun of it. By making them a part of our everyday lifestyle, we can define Christianity, not by what we don't do but by what we do. Invite the children and grandchildren to join in with us. By training, and more important, *showing* our children how to take food baskets to the needy or to do loving deeds for shut-ins, for the sick, or for other children in hospitals and orphanages, the rewards and satisfaction of service to others will powerfully affect their attitudes.

2. Rediscover with them the excitement, wonder, and magic of the child's world. Enjoy! Driving across country intent on getting to our destination, we stopped at a rest area in western Nebraska. Shouts of glee rang out when the kids discovered the swings and teeter-totters. Grandmother, despite her eighty years, went over and began to swing with her grandchildren. Then she giggled at herself. Most of us as we grow older begin selectively to concern ourselves with problems and the burdens of life. Maybe we should lighten up. Do we really need to carry the weight of the world on our shoulders? Yes, the world is terribly wicked and headed for a cataclysm. The time of trouble is coming. But does that mean we can't enjoy the crazy and odd things that flick into our life?

As I [John] was writing this, the squirrel came down the branch near our front picture window, stretched himself down, and hung by his tail as he robbed the bird feeder. I remember the evening I took our grandchild Jenny down the path from the mountain cabin and said, "Now listen carefully, and you'll hear the hoot owl." In silence we waited. Then out of the stillness came, "Whoooooo—whooooo." Her eyes were as big as saucers. The wonder of it all! What childhood days return to your memory? Do you remember the time you saw tadpoles and someone explained to you how they would lose their tails and become frogs? The amazing sight of a rainbow—even a double rainbow? The night you lay on a grassy slope and saw a shooting star and made a wish? You can relive these magic moments with your children and grandchildren, and both you and they will make memories never to be forgotten.

Ever since I [Millie] was a child, Cousin Millie would tell me of how, when she was young and a stewardess for a rich family, they drove to California in their Pierce Arrow car and took the boat to Catalina. Her life had not been brightened by much travel, so we and our children heard this one story over and over again. Then the thought entered our heads, *Why not relive the excitement of her youthful days and pass them on to our children as well?* So when she was ninety, we loaded her, her wheelchair, and walker into our little Honda wagon and headed west. Her fondest memories were relived and retold. We held a family reunion on Catalina Island. She gazed with wonder as our son Wes did handstands on her walker, and both our sons balanced on the two wheels of her wheelchair, keeping the little wheels off the floor! The magic of the past came back to life and was shared with our children.

3. Tell the great stories—the great narratives. Who are the heroes of our children today? In many cases they are rock stars, sports superstars, and TV stars. What a privilege we have of sharing with them the stories of *real* heroes—Daniel in the lions' den, David going up against evil Goliath, Gideon and his three hundred warriors, Paul and Silas singing hymns in prison, Jesus going to Calvary. In the greatest chapter on child rearing in the Bible,

Children Going Home

Deuteronomy 6, verse 20, 21 (NKJV) tells us:

> When your son asks you in time to come, saying, "What is the meaning of the testimonies, the statutes, and the judgments which the LORD our God has commanded you?" then you shall say to your son: "We were slaves of Pharaoh in Egypt, and the LORD brought us out of Egypt with a mighty hand."

In essence, Moses is saying, "Tell them your story. If we don't recount the great narratives, then as far as our children are concerned, they never happened. Tell them the miracles of your life and the miracles of their lives when they were perhaps too young to remember. With tender heart, tell them of how the angels have protected them and saved their lives, because God has something very wonderful for them to do for Him."

We now are creating a family ritual that attempts to retell the story using modern technology. Our son Wes and his family are in Guam and son John and his family live in Ohio. Communication with Wes was a problem, but with his encouragement and insistence, we have gone into cyberspace, and all our immediate family uses e-mail. One thing leads to another. Now part of the weekly routine is for father John to prepare the Friday sunset story for the scattered family. It sometimes takes him two hours to write it all on the computer, and then, because of the international date line, he must do it on Thursday night. But with the pressing of a key, the Friday-night worship story flies into space at the speed of light and is downlinked from a satellite for our children and four grandchildren, who enjoy Grandpa's story even though our families are some ten thousand miles apart. John modernizes Bible stories, putting the names of Jenny, Paul, Dakota, and Madie into the narrative. In the story, they are there when Jesus blesses the children, and He smiles at them and receives the flowers from their hands. Other weeks, the miracle stories of different members of the family are told. So modern miracles of technology can help unite families around the throne of grace, even though geographically they are a half-world apart.

4. *Nurturing the positives while pruning the negatives.* Our children have received good and bad as a legacy. Have you ever bought "weed-and-feed" for your lawn? We need to apply the same principle to ourselves and our families as we do to our gardening. I remember we planted a garden one spring and then left on an extended itinerary. When we returned, our garden was a healthy looking weed patch, with scarcely a choice plant in sight. One spring we planted our garden at the cabin in the mountains of North Carolina. We could not return until late summer. The weeds were so high that even the groundhogs had not found our vegetables. It took three days working with our Weed Eater before we could locate our plants. We have found that our children have a healthy resilience, and, like the garden, they do recover much. But it is so much easier to pull up the brambles and thorns when they are small instead of waiting until they have well-nigh taken over the field. More important, we must spread proper nutrients on the plants. The Bible says, "Do not be overcome by evil, but overcome evil with good" (Rom. 12:21, NKJV). If we water our tender children with love and cultivate them with God's wisdom, by God's grace we and He will be proud of the harvest.

5. *Pray with and for our children.* Prayer moves the arm of omnipotence. The full story of the miracles performed by prayer will never be known until the judgment day. One of our sons once had a friendship with a young woman that was nonbeneficial for both parties. As parents, we dedicated ourselves to "intensive care praying" about this problem. That very week, the friendship broke off. As we enter the decisive last days of earth's history, it is earnest, intercessory prayer

that will turn the hearts of parents to their children and the hearts of children to their parents. The inspired pen has written:

> Parents, help the children. Watch continually to cut off the current, and roll back the weight of evil which is pressing in upon them. The children cannot do this of themselves. Parents can do much. By earnest prayer and living faith they may bind their children upon the altar, and thus secure the watch-care of guardian angels; the guiding hand of God will lead them through the perils of the last days, and bring them off victorious over every foe (*Signs of the Times*, 26 February 1880, 9).

We should confess in prayer our sins, as well as the sins of our children that have alienated them from God. We held a family seminar in a city of the United States, and after the morning session at the potluck dinner, a lady approached me and asked me to pray for her grown daughter, who was living with a man who was not her husband. I felt honored to do this, and as we were searching for a corner of the social hall where there was less noise, the Spirit told me that I should enquire more about the situation and of the woman making this request. So I said, "Before we pray, tell me more about your spiritual situation and your walk with the Lord." Within a couple of minutes, I learned the sad truth that this mother was also living with a man who was not her husband. How could we implore together for the daughter when the mother was alienating the family by the very lifestyle she despised in her daughter?

Thank God, we can do much. By earnest prayer and living faith, we can bind our flesh and blood as gifts to God on the altar. Boldly at the throne of mercy, we can claim forgiveness and the watchcare of guardian angels over our children, even if they are adults and far away. Our prayers cut across the miles at the speed of thought and bring angel messengers to the sides of our children. Our prayers strengthen the powers of the Holy Spirit to work in them repentance and conversion and fill their lives with all the fruit of the Spirit: love, joy, peace, longsuffering, kindness, goodness, faithfulness, gentleness, and self-control.

Cooperating with the Holy Spirit in educating our children

Can you envision your children filled with the Holy Spirit and sharing the final message in the last days? Can you picture your children with you as a united family in the New Jerusalem, waving palms of victory with golden crowns on your heads? Your dream can come true, but by God's grace, you must prepare your children for that destiny. The inspired pen has told us that before the overflowing scourge, we should prepare.

> Gather your children into your own houses; gather them away from those who are disregarding the commandments of God, who are teaching and practicing evil. Get out of the large cities as fast as possible. Establish church schools. Give your children the word of God as the foundation of all their education. This is full of beautiful lessons, and if pupils make it their study in the primary grade below, they will be prepared for the higher grade above (*Testimonies for the Church*, 6:195).

John Amos Comenius, the great Moravian religious educator, had much to say in his epoch-making book *The Great Didactic* about the Holy Spirit and His work in the teaching of our children. Although he lived four hundred years ago, he is recognized by both the secular and religious world as the "First Modern Educator." He said:

Children Going Home

Piety is the gift of God, and is given us from on high by our counsellor and guide, the Holy Spirit. But, since the Holy Spirit usually employs natural agencies, and has chosen parents, teachers, and ministers who should faithfully plant and water the grafts of Paradise, . . . it is right that these should appreciate the extent of their duties (*The Great Didactic*, 218).

Comenius outlined how the Holy Spirit assists leaders of both home and school through guiding them in their work (219). Parents and educators are to seek to receive the gift of "the Holy Ghost, the pledge of our salvation; and that He might thus rule us and preserve us, and, finally, take us to Himself" (230). We are to continually recognize that the part played by the Holy Spirit in our education is indeed wonderful. "For though its first object is to instruct us in things invisible and eternal, it nevertheless unfolds the laws of nature and of art at the same time, teaching us how to reason wisely on all subjects and how to apply our reason in a practical manner" (241).

Results of the Holy Spirit's work on our children

On the day of Pentecost, three thousand souls were convicted that they should follow Jesus. They wanted eternal life, and from the depths of their hearts, parents cried out, " 'Men and brethren, what shall we do?' " Peter answered them: " 'Repent, and let every one of you be baptized in the name of Jesus Christ for the remission of sins; and you shall receive the gift of the Holy Spirit. For *the promise is to you and to your children*" (Acts 2:37-39, NKJV, emphasis supplied).

Peter's sermon on the day of Pentecost announced the partial fulfillment of Joel's Holy Spirit prophecy:

And it shall come to pass in the last days, says God, that I will pour out of my Spirit on all flesh; your sons and your daughters shall prophesy, your young men shall see visions, your old men shall dream dreams. . . . Before the coming of the great and notable day of the Lord. And it shall come to pass that whoever calls on the name of the Lord shall be saved (Acts 2:17, 20, 21).

We still wait for the complete fulfillment of Joel's prophecy. It will come in the latter rain with even greater power than that recorded in Acts.

Bob was a young man from a good Adventist home; he went to school at Mount Vernon Academy in Ohio. In spite of the efforts of God-fearing parents and teachers, he turned his back on the religion of his childhood and rebelled. He ended up expelled from the academy. Musically talented and adventurous, he decided to go to Florida. There he got a job playing in a night club. He felt it was an incredible break when a Hollywood scout came to the night club, observed his talent, and told him to come to Hollywood, where he could get a lucrative job. Dreams of fame and fortune crowded his mind. Not many days after, he loaded his possessions into his car and headed west.

Bob took a motel the first night but couldn't sleep. A battle was waging in his soul. The glittering lights of Hollywood were beckoning, but another Power was drawing him toward home. Not wanting to miss the opportunity of a lifetime, he left the motel in the night and tried to drive west. But the car didn't want to go. Finally, in desperation, he turned the car around, and the motor ran just fine! The darkness of night still hung over the old home place as he drove into the driveway. Surprise! The front light was on. His father met him at the door. "Where is mom?" Bob asked. "Come and see," his father answered. He led Bob upstairs, and there, beside the bed, was his mother kneeling in prayer with the Bible open before her, agonizing with God that He would save their son and bring him back home. Bob found the Lord that night beside his praying parents. His life was completely changed, and he went on to become one of the founders of "Your Story Hour." Who can measure the transforming power of the Holy Spirit?

God's promise was not only for Bob—it is for you and your children. "I will pour My Spirit on your descendants, and My blessing on your offspring" (Isa. 44:3, NKJV).

For your family

1. In family worship, tell the story of your conversion.

2. Also in family worship, share stories of God's providence in protecting the lives of the children when they were young.

3. Start writing a prayer for each child and grandchild. Using the computer makes it easy to insert prayer thoughts. Be specific about character-development areas and needs. Continue to add to the prayer weekly. Underline the parts that indicate an answer to prayer. Evaluate where growth needs to take place and ask God for wisdom and guidance in those areas. Then believe that God is working on behalf of you and your child and that the Holy Spirit and angels are helping you.

4. Fight for your children and grandchildren in intercessory prayer as if their lives depended on it.

5. As parents, set a time this week to study the following references ("For Further Study") and then pray every morning for the next week that the Holy Spirit will intervene in the lives of your children and of the whole family.

For further study

1SM 190—Holy Spirit is the agency to effect conversion of our children.

AH 342—Holy Spirit softens hearts of parents and fits

them for training children.

DA 512—John the Baptist filled with Holy Spirit through prayers of Elizabeth.

LDE (*Last Day Events*) 206—Children proclaim message in last days.

2SM 259—Many little ones laid to rest before time of trouble. Meet and know them in heaven.

LDE 293—Faith of believing parents covers children.

LDE 293—Some little ones are saved whose mothers are lost.

LDE 293—Retarded child saved by grace of God.

LDE 294—Saved pay tribute to faithful mothers.

LDE 293—Resurrected infants wing their way to mothers' arms.

6T 401—Many lost sheep will return to the fold.

21

THE GREAT CONTROVERSY
at the Family Level

(Millie) Satan is at work destroying Christian homes with every trap he can create. Television trash, corrupt movies, sleazy friends, the mystery of sensual iniquity, hereditary tendencies, cultivated habits, irresistible desires, mystic new spirituality, dietary compulsions, drug imprisonments, gambling compulsion, sexual addiction—you name it; Satan has created it. He wants you and your family hopelessly caught up in his web. He has little time to work, so he is going to work with all power and determination to keep you from inhabiting your heavenly mansion. Satan reasons, Why should you and your family enjoy eternal life and happiness when he and his evil angels will not? First Peter 5:8 says, "Be self-controlled and alert. Your enemy the devil prowls around like a roaring lion looking for someone to devour" (NIV). Then Peter tells us in verse 9 to "Resist him, standing firm in the faith" (NIV).

Gloria was a Christian young lady living in Jamaica. She became acquainted with a young man who eventually asked her to marry him. Since he was not a Christian, she refused. Her "friend" then went to a medium and asked that a voodoo curse be placed on Gloria. The incantations began. After several unsuccessful attempts, the medium said, "I see a fence around her, and I can't get to her. There is no curse I can put upon her. I cannot help you."

In Job 1:10, Satan himself recognized that intercessory prayer had made a hedge around Job, his family, and all that he had, on every side. We all need just such a fence of angelic protection every day of our lives. Every child of God is surrounded by a circle of love. No power can penetrate through this circle of love except by permission.

All of us can have the assurance of the mighty power of Jesus Christ for victory and help to overcome Satan's plans to ensnare us. When we choose Christ as the Lord and Saviour of our life—when we choose to have Christ within us and to be part of the kingdom of God, rejecting the kingdom of the world—we are safe. Jesus is strong, all-powerful, omnipotent, and assists us in the battle of the great controversy between good and evil. Without a doubt, we and our family members are caught in a war. We all have been wounded, but victory is in sight.

In every home may be those who have yielded their minds to Satan and are in bondage. But the Bondage Breaker *can* set them free. Underline Luke 4:18, 19 (NIV) in your Bible and read it frequently if there are some in your home who have been enticed by Satan. Jesus says, "The Spirit of the Lord is on me. . . . He has sent me to proclaim freedom for the prisoners. . . . to release the oppressed." Sometimes we try to fight the battle alone. But we can have supernatural help. Rescue squads of angels are in readiness to fight the battle. All they need is an invitation.

Linda's battle

Satan's process of catching, entrapping, and destroying seeks us all. Linda was no exception. It began with the attentions of Bill, a man who had just started attending her local church. His tender blue eyes drew her to wherever he was at church functions. When they conversed, Bill seemed to understand her loneliness, her want for companionship. As time progressed in their friendly, platonic relationship, Linda felt a growing heart desire to be alone with him. They understood each other so well.

Linda sat on a rough boulder near a rushing stream filled with spring snow waters. She was watching children play at the church spring picnic—her children. Her thoughts rambled. *Just one evening. One evening of being special, of being free, of being loved. I can't. I know it is wrong. Terry wouldn't understand. Maybe he wouldn't even care. All he does is sit in front of that dumb television set hour after hour. He wouldn't even miss me. What would Pastor Wilson think if he found out? How would he even know? There are so many church members who aren't faithful—and it all works out. What could I do with the kids? They're too young—they wouldn't know the difference anyway. I could take them over to Mom's and give her some legitimate reason for leaving them for a few hours.*

Linda's pensive thoughts were shattered as she heard her name called. She looked up to see the elderly pastor limping along toward her over the jagged rock. "Linda, I saw you sitting there, staring out into space, and thought I would just like to talk with you while you are alone." He chatted about the children and then looked seriously at Linda. "I've noticed that you and Terry have lost that happy, vibrant spark you had just a few years ago when you, Linda, joined our church congregation. I know it's difficult for you since Terry is not a member of our church, but I have been praying for you and Terry. I firmly believe that God is going to answer my prayers on your behalf."

Linda turned away from Pastor Wilson's quizzical face as he continued. She wished that he would just go away. *This is not the day I want to talk about my marriage or my dysfunctional home. It's like he is reading my inner thoughts.*

Reaching down, the pastor plucked a long blade of grass and twirled it in his fingers. "Linda, there is a Marriage Commitment Seminar this next weekend at Camp Laurelwood. I think you and Terry should attend."

"I don't want to, Pastor. It would just be boring, and besides . . ." As her words trailed off, the pastor insisted, "I think it is so important that I have already made arrangements for you. The way is paid for you and Terry to attend the seminar at the camp."

Determined not to go, Linda tried to remain politely distant. As the dialogue continued, Linda consented to consider attending, breathing a deep inward sigh of relief when the pastor was called to speak to another parishioner. *No way do I want to spend a weekend with Terry at a seminar on marriage. They would probably try to convince me that I have a wonderful husband and that I should be a more faithful wife. That is not what my heart is telling me now. I am tired of this marriage. I just want freedom to . . .*

"Mommie, Mommie, come look at the little fish in the pond!" Her children's voices abruptly invaded her thoughts. *Tomorrow is another day. I will think about it then.*

That Friday afternoon, Linda drove her Honda south toward the camp to attend the not-at-all-desired Marriage Commitment Seminar. Terry, too, drove south after his work so they could arrive on time. He was equally reluctant.

As Linda made her way down the winding roads, a battle raged in her mind. As it got more intense, she spoke bitterly, "God, I don't want to go to this marriage seminar. I don't want to be with Terry, I have lost my love for him—and Bill is so exciting and understanding." And then, in frustration, Linda screamed at God: "God, if you want to save our marriage, You have to change me!" Heaven heard those words.

Terry and Linda met at the camp and found their way to the assigned cabin, talking only when necessary. The program began with enthusiastic leaders commenting about the possibility of having "drag-ees" present, but that they hoped by the end of the seminar all would be pushers, encouraging others to attend the next seminar. Terry and Linda both knew they were drag-ees.

Not looking at each other, sitting almost back to back, detesting to have to write a love letter to each other, Terry and Linda battled through the suggested activities with a group of twenty-two other couples. Time could not pass fast enough until it was over.

It was as if a message were being transmitted to both: *You don't want to be here. This is boring. All this spiritual stuff is not for you. Don't listen to them talk about all those biblical principles about marriage. God doesn't really hate divorce. Just tune out.*

Another voice intruded at the edges of Linda's thoughts. One of the seminar leaders kept saying something about how Satan was intruding in marriages, trying to break up happy husband-and-wife relations, and that people were praying for the destruction of Christian marriages and families. A great controversy was going on between good and evil. It was important to tell Satan, "Get thee behind me. I want no part of your devices and ways of influencing my home and my family members. I don't want to listen to you."

Could this be happening to Terry and me? We did love each other so much when we married. Could it be that Satan is working on our marriage and I am contributing to this evil thing? Am I allowing Satan to work in my marriage through Bill? Am I listening to Satan's subtle voice, and is he enticing me with forbidden fruit?

Linda's victory

Back home, the pastor and his wife gave Terry and Linda prayer cover, specifically praying for the Holy Spirit to work a miracle in their lives and resurrect their dead marriage. Their marriage was so bad that only God could change the situation. While ministering to others and caring for Terry's and Linda's children, the praying team sent dart prayers to the Father to save a precious marriage and family.

During the couple goal-setting time, strange things began to happen between Terry and Linda. There was confession of unmet needs, a discussion of the evils of TV in their home, even communication about their different Christian beliefs. There was a fresh desire on Terry's part to start studying God's Word. Linda could hardly believe her ears. There seemed to be some kind of truce between them. It could perhaps be strangely described as "peace" and maybe "love" again.

If the curtains of heaven had been opened and others could have seen divine agencies at work, a very real battle between good and evil angels would have been visible. There was prayer cover for Terry and Linda, permitting the Holy Spirit and heavenly beings to minister to this couple. Because someone was praying, blessings could be received and help given. God was at work, and prayers were answered.

At the closing session of the Marriage Commitment Seminar, Terry wrote Linda a love letter telling her how much he loved her and needed her. She was the most important person in his life—he would do all he could to bring joy and happiness to her. During the Agape Feast, Terry was able publicly to affirm her in front of the other couples as his eyes overflowed with tears in response to a deep emotion in his heart he had not experienced in a long time. Linda shyly stood, unaware of those about her. She tenderly said, "I am glad God brought you into my life. Tonight I pledge to you that I will be a good wife to you and faithful until death do us part. I love you, Terry." And the Kleenex box was passed around.

And what was the rest of the story? One year later, Linda met the marriage seminar leaders and enthusiastically told what had happened in their lives. "You saved our marriage.

The Great Controversy at the Family Level

We realized that we were allowing Satan to work in our marriage and decided to reject him and invite Jesus to be the head of our home. We have daily devotions, and our family has never been so happy. But the exciting part is that Terry started studying the Bible. Last fall, he was baptized, and I rededicated my life to God and was rebaptized with him. When I told God that He would have to change my life, I didn't have the slightest comprehension of what I was saying. But God took me at my word and performed a miracle in my life and in Terry's; He resurrected a very dead marriage. Thank you for letting God use you to help us."

What Linda and Terry had heard the seminar couple say, the Holy Spirit used and translated it into a powerful and convicting message that changed their lives. All around us, through media and lives of friends and family, we can see evidence for the following statement by Ellen White:

> While men are ignorant of his devices, this vigilant foe is upon their track every moment. He is intruding his presence in every department of the household, in every street of our cities, in the churches, in the national councils, in the courts of justice, perplexing, deceiving, seducing, everywhere ruining the souls and bodies of men, women, and children, breaking up families, sowing hatred, emulation, strife, sedition, murder. And the Christian world seem[s] to regard these things as though God had appointed them and they must exist (*The Great Controversy*, 508).

How God rescued our home from satanic attack

Our story is no different from many where Satan attempts to destroy relationships and cause dysfunction and a mountain of problems. When John's wife died, leaving him with two sons, he felt the need not only for another mother for his sons (ages eleven and thirteen) but also for a wife to love him and to be his companion. Our courtship and marriage were full of beautiful memories, but after that, the blending of two families was not like a dream but more like a nightmare. Being a new mother for two active and strong-willed children was demanding, difficult, and far more complex than I had anticipated. Although we had daily devotions and chose Christ as the center of our home, we encountered lots of problems—misunderstandings were frequent. At times no one seemed happy. The adjustment was not easy.

During this time, John left to teach at an extension school in Mexico. I was left alone with the children. John told me not to rock the boat too much with the children—he would be back soon. It was an arduous time. I had an extremely heavy teaching load. The sons were pushing boundaries, and I was beginning to wonder where I could turn my "mother" button in. One night, tired and exhausted, I tried to sleep. I couldn't. My mind began to wander, and a new thought came into my head, "You don't love John anymore." Startled, I thought, *Where did that come from?* After thinking more of my problems, I dozed off to a fitful rest. The next day was another exhausting day, full of not only my problems but everyone else's. The children had not improved, and I was at my wit's end. That night as I tried to have some devotions, the same thought returned to my mind. *You don't love John anymore.*

Suddenly I realized the source of that thought and said out loud so that Satan could hear me, "I *do* love John. Get thee behind me, Satan. I reject that thought." Never again has that thought returned, and I praise God for it.

Our problems continued, but God was changing all of our characters in the family through them—we all needed each other. There have been a number of occasions where we have covenanted as a family to strive for the kingdom of God and the goal of an eternal home. That is still our goal.

The Great Controversy at the Family Level

Our characters have improved, and we are still growing—God is not through with us yet. We all realize how Satan has tried to ensnare us, but our prayer is that with God's help, we will all be strong and faithful.

Meeting insinuations of the enemy

Satan does not blunder in like a bull in a China closet. He slithers in like a snake in the grass. He introduces his tempting thoughts to anyone who will yield to them. Once people find themselves on the enemy's territory, it is difficult to find the way back home. The devil gives us thoughts just as he did to Judas and David. He is extremely deceptive. Sometimes he will suggest they should get a divorce—and they even believe that these thoughts come from God. But we have a defense. Simply say, "Get thee behind me, Satan. And, God, I don't know how to handle all of my problems, but I know You can help me/us."

When people open themselves to following Satan's subtle suggestions, he takes control of lives and truly controls minds—then he has a stronghold. To break the stronghold he has, we have to have a desire for Satan to be expelled from our lives. The Bible has to be studied in the areas dealing with our temptations—and its counsel turned into prayers. This was Christ's method of meeting temptation. He fought Satan with " 'It is written, "Man shall not live by bread alone." ' " Christ won. Record God's promises and turn them into prayers. Write prayers to God and talk to the Father orally, at home, or as you drive or walk. Communicate constantly until there is victory. Other suggestions: get counsel or invite people to pray for you.

A lady who had been involved with a musical group focusing on satanism was blind at first to the true nature of the performances. Later God broke through and gave her insight, and she reported that before each performance, someone would say, "Let's go plant seed." That was seed for

Satan. Satan's work is to kill, steal, and destroy. He is pleased when he has many helpers and when thousands and millions uncritically swallow his suggestions.

Dave Wilkerson was encouraged to go to a Christian rock concert and was assured that it was acceptable. After being there a short time, he realized that the performance was not of God. The room was filled with smoke. As he was praying for spiritual discernment, it was as if his eyes were opened. He saw that the place was filled with demons.

Some in even Christian families are not aware of the seed being sown in their own homes by television programs, musical tapes, and satanic games children play on game boards or the computer. Increasingly children find access on the Worldwide Web to pornography and young people have intimate conversations on the Internet with people whose character they know nothing about. Can we imagine that the planting of this seed will yield no harvest?

One mother said that when she looked out of her home into the world, she could not let her children leave the doors of home without a protecting prayer hedge of angels over and around them. She continued to pray all day long for her children. There are other homes where parents, children, friends, and relatives willingly invite rebel forces into the embassy house of the heavenly government, where there should be a safe harbor.

A Christian on a flight observed that a seatmate was not eating. The seatmate said he was fasting. "I am pleased that you are praying to the Lord," the Christian responded. "Not so," the other answered. "I am a satanist fasting and praying for the destruction of marriages." Another report tells of a prayer breakfast where satanists were praying that ministers' marriages would be destroyed. If satanists are fasting and praying, how diligent should we be to counteract their evil work and to give prayer cover and protection to Christian families—especially to ministers who daily have to give battle to the enemy.

An excellent book that will help those who desire greater insight into the battle between good and evil is *Bondage Breaker*, by Neil T. Anderson. It seems to take a balanced approach. A caution: Some who read about spiritual warfare begin to be so obsessed with the devil and his power they forget the power of Christ that gained the victory over our evil enemy on Calvary.

The books of Roger Morneau are *must* reading for those desiring to learn the skills of intercessory praying for your family. His stories illustrate answers to prayer and tell of how our God is alive and well—of how He hears and answers prayer. *Incredible Answers to Prayer, More Incredible Answers to Prayer*, and *When You Need Incredible Answers to Prayer* are excellent reading and are faith-building.

Satan's agenda versus God's agenda

Satan has a short time to work. His two points of great emphasis are the institutions established in Eden—the Sabbath and marriage. His great goals are to:

Destroy Sabbath rest
Destroy marriages
Destroy families
Destroy society
Destroy churches

Daniel O'Ffill, in his book *What to Say in a Whole New Way*, writes of Satan and his angels having a council to see how they can more effectively work against God's children. He writes:

Let's imagine Satan talking with his angels. Satan says, "We lost in heaven. We lost at Calvary. But we can win in the judgment of the living, before the return of Christ."

His angels ask, "What can we do to win?"

Satan answers, "Go out over the earth and bring pressure to bear on all Christians. Keep them all sinning. Keep them breaking God's commandments, for which we were cast out of heaven because we disobeyed them. Then if, in His judgment of the living, Christ designates just one person for translation who is not obedient as well as repentant, He must take all of us back to heaven too!" (25).

We as families have a great work to do as we team up with heavenly agencies to set the captives free. Read Luke 4:18, 19 for the commission. Young and old can help release those in bondage.

A sixth-grader was taking part in a "Ten Days of Prayer" intensive during the first days of January and was concerned for one person who had asked for prayer. When the group divided up for intercession by different categories, this young child requested to join the group praying specifically for the person in bondage. She earnestly prayed in faith, "Jesus, You freed people before—You can do it again." And He does!

For your family

1. Why is it that some families have so many problems and others have it so easy?

2. What spiritual battles are taking place in your own family? What measures and strategies are you using to combat the enemy and assure victory?

3. We are wrestling against principalities and powers. Read Eph. 6:12 and discuss what this text is saying to your family.

4. Christ has won the victory. Through Him we have freedom and help. Search together for Bible verses and quotations from Ellen White that confirm this. Here are three verses

to get you started. Share your findings.

Jude 24: "Now to Him who is able to keep you from stumbling, and to present you faultless before the presence of His glory with exceeding joy" (NKJV).

2 Corinthians 5:17, 18: "Therefore, if anyone is in Christ, he is a new creation; old things have passed away; behold, all things have become new. Now all things are of God, who has reconciled us to Himself through Jesus Christ" (NKJV).

1 Corinthians 15:57: "But thanks be to God, who gives us the victory through our Lord Jesus Christ" (NKJV).

5. Pray concerning personal sins and ask forgiveness of each other and of God. Discuss the theme with your family: "When we have messed up, confession with true repentance takes back the ground given to Satan."

6. We are encouraged to put on the whole armor of God—Ephesians 6:13-17 and 2 Corinthians 10:3, 4. What is this armor, and how can it help our family to go home to the mansions prepared for us?

7. "Resist the devil and he will flee from you," we are told in James 4:7 (NKJV). Without telling anyone else but God, share with Him areas where you need strength to resist the devil in your daily life and character. Then ask Him for help and claim the promise of Isaiah 41:10.

8. Pray for the marriages in your church, and especially for the minister and his or her family. They need your prayers. But most of all pray for love, harmony, acceptance, and God's blessing for your own family.

CHAPTER
22

YOUR FAMILY
and the Scarlet Beast

If you heard that a ferocious beast was on its way to attack and destroy your family, would you take notice? If you were then told on good authority that no human power could stop this hideous beast and that in the whole universe there was only one being who could thwart the impending doom, would you be alarmed? And then suppose you were to learn that this terror had systematically invaded every human power of this world and the spirit world—what would you feel then? This is the plot we are looking at in this chapter. But first, some biblical background.

Babylon the Great

Babylon, the seat of a kingdom that raised its might against the people of God, sat on the River Euphrates. This great urban center fell in 539 B.C. when Cyrus the Persian diverted the river and overcame the city. A series of Persian decrees then invited the exiled Jews to come out of Babylon. This message was emphasized by prophets as well, warning the Israelites to escape from the city. A similar message, using other motifs, was given repeatedly in the Bible: Noah and his family were called to come out of a wicked world and into the ark of safety; Abraham was called to come out of Mesopotamia to the Promised Land; Lot was called to come out of Sodom; the children of Israel were called to come out of Egypt; and finally, in Revelation, the people of God are called to come out of a Babylonian lifestyle of sin and death to eternal life.

The point of these "calling out" messages, as well as many other biblical narratives, was not primarily geographical. *It was a message of deliverance from bondage, slavery, and death into the freedom of worshiping and walking with the true God.* God's first interest has never been in real estate but rather in the *experience* of His chosen people. He desires His people to be free from sin, decay, and death. Take Elijah's dramatic call to all Israel on Mt. Carmel. It was a call to turn their backs on Baal worship and to turn their hearts in repentance to God through the merits of an innocent sacrifice. It was a succinctly experiential, rather than a geographical, priority call. So all through history, the question is repeated: Whom will we obey and follow? Will it be the creature or the Creator? Man or God? Jesus in His mission statement at Nazareth stated that the Spirit of the Lord "has sent Me to heal the brokenhearted, to preach deliverance to the captives and recovery of sight to the blind, to set at liberty those who are oppressed" (Luke 4:18, NKJV). Our God has no pleasure in seeing people die—He longs for all to turn from death and live (Eze. 18:31, 32).

The symbols of the last Babylon

In the midst of Revelation's incredibly rich imagery, where the events of a not-so-distant end are symbolically portrayed, there are two entities we would like to concentrate on. The first is pictured initially as a leopardlike beast (13:1-10), then as a harlot (17:1-6), and then as a great city (17:18)—this represents papal Rome. The second is pictured as supporting the harlot, either as waters (17:1), or as a scarlet beast

(17:3). This second entity represents "peoples, multitudes, nations, and tongues" (17:15)—all of whom follow and worship the world's system and reject God's authority. Notice that the harlot sits on the scarlet beast. A support system is definitely indicated. While organizations pawn off error onto the earth, the people like this error and support it—it is apparently quite appealing to the natural heart. The prophet Jeremiah (5:30, 31, NKJV) said it well: "An astonishing and horrible thing has been committed in the land: the prophets prophesy falsely, and the priests rule by their own power; and My people love to have it so." It is ultimately the people who support the evil systems. They "love to have it so."

This is our point. The final apostasy will be a total world system—people confederated against God and His Word. This total world system will have "one mind" (Rev. 17:13, 17). It will be a complete world system—political, legislative, military, economic, philosophical, psychological, educational, scientific—which will combine in a universal, one-minded "groupthink" never before known in history. Our only defense will be to think as the Word of God wants us to think. This great deception will include the financial powers of Wall Street, Tokyo, and the European Economic Community; the mass media czars of radio, television, and the press; the philosophies of post-modernism, behaviorism, pragmatism, idealism, and realism; the cultural systems of Hollywood and Paris and even the tribalism of remote areas.

The web of final apostasy will include the economics of industrialism and the distribution of commercialism—and people who cross every ethnic line, language, and dialect known to man. The political power of the United Nations, the United States, and every nation on the globe—all will join together in a cataclysmic "group think" to coerce the conscience and to lead individuals away from a total reliance upon the Word of God. This geo-megasystem will unite to support and carry spiritual deceptions headed by mother

Your Family and the Scarlet Beast

Rome and trumpeted by an apostate Protestantism that no longer protests. It will embrace the spiritual intensity of the religious right, the liberalism of the religious left, the miracle workers of the New Age, charismatics and spiritists, as well as animism and ancestor worship.

Every earthly power will unite to wipe God's commandment-keeping, loyal remnant off the planet. It will be a battle between knowledge of the world and knowledge of the Word— a battle between the dying and the living. The total world system will, in effect, be saying, "You are strange. You are different. You don't belong here. You've got to go!" In a sense, they are right. We don't belong here. We are citizens of another country—a heavenly one. Our every earthly support will be removed by means of economic boycott, a death decree, and universal excommunication from society (*The Great Controversy*, 615). We will realize that what Paul says is right: "the form of this world is passing away" (1 Cor. 7:31, NKJV). We will crave for reunion with Christ, who said, "They are not of the world. . . . Father, I desire that they also whom You gave Me may be with Me where I am" (John 17:16, 24, NKJV).

Can you imagine what it will mean to have every academic, scientific, economic, military, political, and mass-media dimension of the planet arrayed against you and your family's loyalty to God? That is what it will cost to be "out of Babylon"—out of step—in the last days. What relationship we will need with our children, what strength of mind, what rootedness in the Word of God, what individuality to be able to think and act on conscientious principle rather than go with the "one-mindedness"—the "group think"—of a whole world system! That is the challenge. Will we live by the Word of God or by the word of Babylon? All the crises of all the ages—the moral crisis before the Flood, the fiery furnace the three Hebrew worthies faced, the death decree faced by Queen Esther and her people, and the persecutions of the

1260-year time period—they are all put into one last package for the grand finale. There will be only one way out.

Your family and the Lamb

Notice what the Scripture says. The all-encompassing human powers "will make war with the Lamb, and the Lamb will overcome them, for He is Lord of lords and King of kings; and those who are with Him are called, chosen, and faithful" (Rev. 17:14, NKJV). Who is this Lamb? He is "The Word of God" (Rev. 19:13). He is the same Lamb presented in Revelation 5:6 "as though it had been slain [Calvary], having seven horns [perfect power], and seven eyes [complete knowledge, intelligence, insight]" and who is the only One in the cosmos who is worthy and has prevailed to open the scroll of history and the future. He is the only One who knows everything about your family—where you came from, the factors that interplay in the character formation of each son and daughter, and how you can cooperate to save them. He is the One whose redeeming sacrifice was planned by the Trinity "from the foundation of the world" and who holds the Book of Life in His nail-pierced hand that contains the name of each member of your family if they have accepted His sacrifice (Rev. 13:8). He is the only power in the universe who can wash our past lives white in His blood (Rev. 7:14). He is the only force who can successfully confront—and defeat—the scarlet beast.

In the Lamb, your family is victorious

The Lamb: He is the One who sits on the throne with the power to give salvation and hope to those who accept His victory and accept the clean, white robe of His righteousness (Rev. 7:9, 10). You see, it is already positively certain. The Lamb is going to completely overcome the scarlet beast representing the teeming millions who support the Babylonian world system. If we choose the Lamb, we will overcome with Him. If we choose the world system and Babylon, we will be vanquished with them. If we choose the Lamb, we will sing the Song of Moses and of the Lamb[1] when we stand on the sea of glass having the harps of God (Rev. 15:2, 3). With the victorious Lamb, we can stand on Mt. Zion having the Father's name—His character—written in our foreheads, and we can "follow the Lamb wherever He goes" (Rev. 14:1, 4, NKJV). He will eternally shield us from hunger and thirst, "for the Lamb who is in the midst of the throne will shepherd them and lead them to living fountains of waters" (Rev. 7:17, NKJV). If our family chooses to remain in Babylon, we will be part of the world system that hides at His coming and that calls to the mountains and rocks, "Fall on us and hide us from the face of Him who sits on the throne and from the wrath of the Lamb!" (Rev. 6:16, 17, NKJV). But as a part of His victorious church, we will be invited to the marriage of the Lamb and the marriage supper (Rev. 19:7, 9). We, our spouse, and our children as overcomers will inherit all things and will sit down in the throne of the Lamb with Him as co-rulers of the universe (Rev. 21:7; 3:21).

Too good to be true?

Does it all seem too good to be true? Mind-boggling? Overwhelming? Frightening? Be of good cheer. On the night of His betrayal, Christ said, "Be of good cheer, I have overcome the world" (John 16:33, NKJV). When by faith we hang our helpless souls and the eternal welfare of our children on Him, His victory on the cross will be ours. Revelation 12:11 tells us three ways we can be overcomers in Him.

1. "And they overcame him [Satan] by the blood of the Lamb" (NKJV). There is no other way we can claim pardon for our past and victory for the present and the future—only in the blood of Jesus. Yet like the blood of the Passover, it is not enough to have the blood in the basin—it needed to be painted on the doorposts of their houses and the Lamb had to be eaten. In our lives, it is not enough to say that the blood of Jesus did it all. That blood needs to be applied in our family, in our lifestyle—we *live* by every word that proceeds out of the mouth of God.

2. "And they overcame . . . by the word of their testimony" (NKJV). The victor's crown in heaven is for those who overcome, who by the testimony of their mouths and their lives honor the One who died on the cross for them. For those who have passed from death unto life, the most natural thing in the world will be to give testimony to others of God's saving grace in their lives.

3. "And they did not love their lives to the death" (NKJV). The bottom line is *loyalty*. Will we be loyal to the Babylonian system and the rebel masses who support it? Or will we be loyal to the Lamb who died for us? Contemplating Jesus' marvelous sacrifice for us, duty becomes a delight and sacrifice a pleasure. No sacrifice would be too great, even death itself, if it would glorify the One who gave His all for us.

For your family

1. Write a prayer of allegiance to God. Allow your thoughts on loyalty and victory to crystallize fully, and then share them in family worship.

In the prayer, tell Christ how much His death for your sins means to you. Ask God to help you be an overcomer.

Praise God for His goodness to you and tell Jesus how much you love Him. Make this prayer a masterpiece—it might take a week to write.

Ask God to help your family be loyal and strong during the difficult and triumphant days of this world's history.

---

1. Both symbolize victory. The Song of Moses was to celebrate victory after the Red Sea and desert experience, and the Song of the Lamb celebrates eternal victory.

CHAPTER

23

THE FAMILY'S LAST CALL

"'Elijah truly is coming first and will restore all things'"
(Matt. 17:11, NKJV).

Drought and famine grip the land nearly nine centuries before Christ. Almost all the cattle are dead. Thousands of children are dying from malnutrition and starvation. King Ahab and his royal court ascend the sun-parched slope of Mount Carmel. Four hundred fifty prophets of Baal take their place around the altar of their god. Close behind them, beneath the now leafless trees of their grove, stand four hundred prophets of Asherah, surrounding the sacred wooden statue of their goddess of fertility.

Opposite this imposing retinue stands one lone man—his dress simple, his features rugged. His name, *Elijah*, given him by unknown parents of the eastern province of Gilead, means "Jehovah is my God." He stands beside a broken-down altar of twelve stones. Years ago, families used to worship there, before the Baal altars became so popular.

Elijah speaks, and his voice echoes to the tens of thousands in Israel who have gathered on the ridges and in the valley below. " 'How long will you go limping with two different opinions? If the Lord is God, follow Him; but if Baal, then follow him' " (1 Kings 18:21, RSV). The word *Baal* means "lord." The religion of Baal—corrupted by immorality, drunkenness, and gross idolatry—negated everything Jehovah commanded.

The pagan priests build an altar for Baal, and an impressive and sophisticated ceremony takes place. They speak beautiful words, and ecstatic rites follow. No one could question that Baal's devotees believe in their god. They are willing to shed their own blood to prove it. But, there is no fire—no power! After about six hours of frantic calling on Baal, jumping around the altar, and cutting themselves with knives, silence descends upon the mountain. The prophets of Baal are hoarse, bleeding, exhausted. There is still no fire—no sign that any god hears. They retire from the contest.

Isn't that the way it is when one worships other gods—even the popular ones of this late twentieth century? Man is a worshiping creature. He is always worshiping someone or something. If it's not the true God, he will find a substitute—maybe even himself.

At the hour of the evening sacrifice, Elijah steps forward. As he surveys much of the nation of Israel, his eyes seem to pierce their souls. In their faces, he reads the tragic stories of those who have sought for happiness at other altars, who have worshiped money, lust, prestige, and pleasure. He sees the childless arms of mothers who have sacrificed the lives of their children for the "good life" of their culture. The broken marriages and the broken hearts that fill the country meet his gaze.

His great heart yearns in love for the deluded people. They have gone into the deepest apostasy in the history of Israel. They are following Jezebel. Spiritually, the people are bankrupt and have sunk to the depths of the Canaanites before them. They have institutionalized the repulsive child sacrifice and sex worship of the god Baal and the goddess

The Family's Last Call

Asherah. In invitation, Elijah stretches out his arms and asks them to approach him. "So all the people came near to him. And he repaired the altar of the Lord that was broken down" (verse 30, NKJV). The way back to God begins with the repairing of the abandoned altar. It was time for the people to come out of their apostasy and turn their hearts toward home.

Is it not time now to heed Elijah's message and rebuild our family altars for heart-turning within our homes?

What will happen when altars are rebuilt?

The scene that follows the rebuilding of the altar on Mount Carmel is one of the most dramatic in Bible history. Elijah offers a prayer. Not flowery or complicated, it is only about thirty seconds long. See the prophet kneeling beside the altar, hands outstretched. He pleads the merits of the blood to cover the sins of the people. "And it came to pass at the time of the offering of the evening sacrifice, that Elijah the prophet came near, and said, Lord God of Abraham, Isaac, and of Israel, let it be known this day that thou art God in Israel. . . . Hear me, O Lord, hear me, that this people may know that thou art the Lord God, and that thou hast *turned their heart* back again" (1 Kings 18:36, 37, KJV, emphasis supplied).

"Then the fire of the Lord fell." The marvel of the story is that the fire, instead of falling on the sinful people, fell upon the innocent victim. The shed blood of Jesus claimed at that altar covered the sinners and permitted the penitent to respond: "The Lord, He is the God; the Lord, He is the God" (verse 39, KJV).

Today, the TV altar has displaced the family altar in millions of homes. Parents wonder why they find no fire, no power, in their spiritual lives, why temptation so easily overcomes their children. Parents must sense the dangers their children face. We need to claim the victory available for our families in the blood of Christ. Ministering angels will guard our children when we have thus dedicated them to God. The consecrating fire of God will fall upon such dedicated children, and the showers of the latter rain upon worshiping families. Then all will know that Jehovah is God and there is none else. And remember—it all begins with a father and mother who repair "the altar of the Lord that was broken down."

God is *measuring* our personal and family devotions. "Then I was given a reed like a measuring rod. And the angel stood, saying, 'Rise and measure the temple of God, the altar, and those who worship there' " (Revelation 11:1, NKJV). As a family on earth gathers around their altar, they enter by faith into the Holy of Holies in heaven. As His earthly children claim the merits of His blood, Jesus Himself presents their petitions before His Father and covers them with the white robe of His grace. Is this work of Jesus somehow related to last-day prophecies mentioned in scripture?

The investigative judgment in Malachi

"Behold, I send My messenger to prepare the way before me, and the Lord whom you seek will suddenly come to his temple; the messenger of the covenant in whom you delight, behold, he is coming, says the Lord of hosts" (Malachi 3:1, RSV).

What does "*the Lord whom you seek will suddenly come to his temple*" mean? What does "His temple" refer to? This refers to Christ's coming to "the most holy place for the work of the investigative judgment" (*SDA Bible Commentary*). The first angel's message, of Revelation 14:6, 7, proclaims this momentous event prophesied in Daniel 8:14 and Malachi 3:1-5. (See *The Great Controversy*, 424, 426, 480).

The "messenger of the covenant" refers to Jesus, who comes before the Father in the second and final phase of His heavenly priestly ministry. But there are two messengers in Malachi 3:1. To whom does "My messenger" refer?

The Family's Last Call

"My messenger"

The name of the prophet Malachi literally means "My messenger." This is the theme of the book. The message culminates in the Elijah message of chapter 4:5, 6. God sends "My messenger" before His face. Christ comes twice to the earth. Before the appearance of Royalty, the messenger comes to announce His coming. This was also prophesied by Isaiah:

> The voice of one crying in the wilderness; prepare the way of the Lord; make straight in the desert a highway for our God. Every valley shall be exalted, and every mountain and hill shall be made low; the crooked places shall be made straight, and the rough places smooth; the glory of the Lord shall be revealed (Isaiah 40:3-5, NKJV).

Before the first coming, God sent John the Baptist as His messenger. The angel Gabriel announced to Zacharias before the birth of John that " 'he will turn many of the children of Israel to the Lord their God. He will also go before Him in the spirit and power of Elijah, "to turn the hearts of the fathers to the children," and the disobedient to the wisdom of the just, to make ready a people prepared for the Lord.' " The angel Gabriel's words in Luke 1:16, 17 (NKJV) are quoting Malachi 4:5, 6. The first prophecy of New Testament times picks right up 430 years later, just where the last prophecy of Old Testament times left off. When John began preaching in the Wilderness of Judea, he quoted Isaiah 40:3-5 as his credentials. He was " 'the voice of one crying in the wilderness: "Prepare the way of the Lord" ' " (Luke 3:4-6, NKJV).

God will not leave Himself without a witness when Christ returns the second time in the clouds of heaven. Again, the "messenger" goes before His face. The Elijah message meets its total and final fulfillment, preparing a people for "the great and terrible day of the Lord" (Mal. 4:5, RSV).

Great events in heaven call for corresponding great events on earth. Let us illustrate this point by two episodes in history and one present-future event.

1. *Heaven*—When Christ ascended to heaven, the inauguration ceremony lasted ten days. The oil of anointing was poured on Jesus (Psa. 133:1, 2), and He was fully installed as high priest ministering in the Holy Place of the heavenly sanctuary. A great event was taking place in heaven, and it called for a corresponding great event on earth.

Earth—At that precise moment, the oil figuratively fell to the earth. The Holy Spirit descended on the waiting disciples, who had put away all their differences and were in one accord. The result: Pentecost.

2. *Heaven*—In 1844, Christ inaugurated the second phase of His ministry in the Most Holy Place of the heavenly sanctuary. This momentous event was destined to culminate the great controversy and make up the jewels of Christ's kingdom. As stated in Malachi 3:1-5, the Messenger of the covenant came suddenly to His temple to refine, purify, and purge. He came to be a swift witness against sorcerers, adulterers, perjurers, exploiters, and those who don't live what they profess. A great event was taking place in heaven, and it called for a corresponding great event on earth.

Earth—The result on earth was the Midnight Cry—one of the greatest religious revivals since the days of the apostles. Thus it is in Malachi 3:1 that "My messenger"—Elijah's message (Mal. 4:5, 6)—would proclaim to the earthly family the momentous events that concern them, that are being accomplished at that time by the heavenly family.

3. *Heaven*—In the present-future, Christ is finishing His high priestly work. Soon the solemn words will be pronounced in heaven: "He who is unjust, let him be unjust still; he who is filthy, let him be filthy still; he who is righteous, let him be righteous still; he who is holy, let him be holy still" (Rev. 22:11, NKJV). This will be the final judicial announcement,

as Jesus forever lays aside His priestly intercessory robes and clothes Himself in His kingly robes to return to earth to save His waiting ones and execute judgment on those who have refused so great a salvation. Great events in heaven call for corresponding great events on earth.

Earth—The Three Angels' Messages (Revelation 14:6-12) must warn every inhabitant of earth. The Elijah message must "prepare the way of the Lord, and make His paths straight!" (Luke 3:4, NKJV). It must "turn the hearts of the fathers to the children and the hearts of the children to their fathers" "before the coming of the great and dreadful day of the Lord" (Malachi 4:6, 5, NKJV).

Yes, the hour of God's judgment has come (Revelation 14:7). As Jesus ministers the benefits of His atonement, we need to be in daily touch with the cosmic issues about us. As the Messenger of the covenant (Jesus) ministers for us, the other messenger, Elijah (the first one mentioned in Malachi 3:1, KJV), must do his work on earth—"and he shall *prepare the way* before me." Isaiah said: "The voice of him that crieth in the wilderness, Prepare ye the way of the Lord, make straight in the desert a highway for our God. . . . The crooked shall be made straight, and the rough places plain: and the glory of the Lord shall be revealed" (40:3-5, KJV).

Elijah himself does not reappear. The one who prepared the way for the first coming of Jesus was John the Baptist. He disclaimed being the reincarnation of Elijah (John 1:21), yet he did a mighty work "in the spirit and power of Elijah" (Luke 1:17, RSV), restoring all things and preparing the way for the first coming of Christ. Now, at the end of the age, "before the coming of the great and dreadful day of the Lord," a mighty work must take place. Elijah himself will not reappear. Those who expect him will be as disappointed as were the literalist Jews who rejected John. But a prophetic message goes forth, proclaimed "in the spirit and power of Elijah." Its purpose will be to restore *all things*—every institution marred by sin—back to their original beauty. All will be reset in the lives of God's chosen as a witness to His glory—marriage, the family, the Sabbath. Each will occupy the place and fulfill the function that God intended:

"And they that shall be of thee shall build the old waste places: thou shalt raise up the foundations of many generations; and thou shalt be called, The repairer of the breach, The restorer of paths to dwell in" (Isaiah 58:12, KJV).

God's people will restore the breach in both the Sabbath and the family commandments. They will reset the two beautiful gifts entrusted to man in Eden, like jewels in God's jewel case.

A prophetic message

The Seventh-day Adventist message is a message of prophecy. We are a prophetic people. We are called out of Babylon—out of its confusion and apostasy—to restore broken relationships and make ready a people to meet their God. A part of this prophecy is that it will restore the Sabbath of the fourth commandment. This is one Eden institution. Another part of the prophecy is that during this investigative judgment in heaven, it will restore the family institution here on earth, "turning the hearts of the fathers to the children and the children to their fathers." The Adventist message is to be characterized by its restoration of the second Eden institution—marriage and the family—to its rightful place. These are important credentials. *We should be just as well known as family restorers as we are as Sabbath restorers.*

Sin, which is basically the breaking of relationships, will be put away under this mighty message. Marriage oneness will be restored; alienated children and parents will draw together; broken hearts will be healed.

Heart turning in our family

We will never forget the vacation our family took at Ouray, Colorado. We had been married just a short time, and the boys and Millie were trying to adjust to each other. The scenery was beautiful, but at our campsite, all was not well. Everybody was mad at everybody else. It was Sabbath, and whatever could go wrong already had. After a bad night in which she slept but little, Millie felt tempted to turn in her "mother" button. The four of us hiked in silence up a mountain trail to have our Sabbath service together. It began to rain, and we sought shelter under a big pine tree. There, pressed together by Mother Nature, we finally began to communicate. We spoke about our common desire to understand each other better.

After a few minutes, John suggested we form a circle and pray for each other. John and Millie, John Jr., and Wes all prayed. Parent and child said they were sorry—and the hearts of the parents turned to their children and the hearts of the children turned to their parents. Tears flowed. In our circle, we made a family covenant that come what may, we would stay loyal as a family to each other and that by God's grace we would journey together to the heavenly Canaan. All our problems weren't miraculously solved in that moment, but that family covenant represented a turning point for our family. We thank God that through thick and thin, we are basically united, and by God's grace we are headed toward heaven.

"Behold, I will send you Elijah the prophet before the coming of the great and dreadful day of the Lord: And he shall *turn the heart of the fathers to the children, and the heart of the children to their fathers*, lest I come and smite the earth with a curse" (Malachi 4:5, 6, NKJV, emphasis supplied). Isn't it time for us to come out of the apostasy of false priorities and the Baals and Asherahs of today? God calls us to come out of these heart-breaking experiences that can never bring us peace. He invites us to turn our hearts to our spouse, our children, our parents, and together to turn our faces toward home.

For your family

1. Do you as a family have a love-focus that places God second? Do you love anything more than God?

2. Read 1 Kings 18:17-46. What message does the Lord have for your family in this story? Which of the following might be gods[1] in your home?

——ambition ——movies ——housework
——sports ——money ——church work
——pleasure ——education ——entertainment
——rock music ——friends ——TV
——fashions ——popularity ——possessions
——work ——jewelry ——other_____

3. Before Elijah started rebuilding the altar, he said, "Come near to me" (1 Kings 18:30). What can you do as a family to "come near" to each other so your family worship and living will be more meaningful?

4. *Prophets and Kings*, pages 144-154, may be read as a continuous story for three to four worships. How can you start to build or rebuild your family altar?

A. Will family worship be daily? _____
B. Will family worship be morning and evening? _____
C. What time in the morning?_____
      In the evening? _____
D. How long will worship last?_____
E. Who will be responsible for worship?

	Sun.	Mon.	Tue.	Wed.	Thurs.	Fri.	Sab.
Morning	____	____	____	____	____	____	____
Evening	____	____	____	____	____	____	____

F. To start with, what worship materials do you wish to use?

5. Just for interest and evaluation, how many hours does each family member spend watching TV?

The Family's Last Call

Name	Hours per Day	Hours per Week
_____	_____	_____
_____	_____	_____
_____	_____	_____
_____	_____	_____
_____	_____	_____

Are you satisfied with the amount? If not, what can each person do to change?

---

1. A god is someone or something that keeps us from worshiping Jesus with the whole heart. Do we love some of the above more than we love God?

CHAPTER

24

DON'T THEY WANT TO COME HOME?

Acrid smoke drifts up from the trash burning in yet another metal drum on a corner. Nameless and faceless bodies huddle over it, stretching out their hands over feeble flames. They are not noticed. Cold streaks of light still hover over metal roofs—the last evidences of a sun that has finished another seemingly empty day. There is no snow. Winter here has only a creeping cold. The body next to the subway entrance shifts slightly, turning toward the wall and away from the wind.

A world away—two city blocks—two thirty-somethings pause in their fiscal planning for a planned evening out with a group of friends. A local restaurant, some good food, a few drinks, good music. They head toward the subway, past the derelicts, around the trash barrel and the drunk sleeping by the subway entrance, all as much a part of the city landscape as the concrete. The thirty-somethings disappear down into the tunnels, as faceless and nameless as the derelicts they don't see.

In another city, two figures walk silently together. Warm, rich colors of evening wash over housetops and golden city streets. They walk as old friends do, shoulders touching occasionally. They are surrounded by an environment obviously planned by master urban designers intent on celebrating the human element. Beauty, grace, texture, material—all are blended in incredible composition. The landscape boasts exotic ground cover and trees, parks that almost beg children to play in them, and benches inviting friends to sit and talk. But it is empty. The footsteps of the two figures echo eerily between the graceful buildings. There are no other names and no other faces making this beautiful city a home. The beauty that is so strong here seems inextricably bound to the ugly emptiness of the first city—one filled with homeless, faceless lives; the other filled with achingly empty homes without life.

The echoes of footsteps fall still. One figure, the Master, stands looking at the emptiness around them. The other, Gabriel, looks at the pain on his Master's face, and breaks the silence:

"The beauty here is beyond description. Only You could create such perfection."

"It would be beautiful," answered the Master, "if it were not so empty."

Silence returns to the two. The Master continues walking, and Gabriel follows after a moment.

"Master, didn't You hope to bring them home long before this?"

"Yes . . ." The one simple word seems to deepen the sadness. The Master pauses and bends to sit on a child's bench, feeling the living wood with His hands. Gabriel strides up to Him, pent-up feelings spilling out.

"Master, You, of all of us, know what it is like for them there. You have seen it. So many have no homes at all, living in the streets, or in overcrowded hovels. The others have walls and ceilings over them, and they hunger to find security in their houses, but their hearts are as empty as those with no homes. None of us can understand it. Why, when they want a home and security so badly, do they refuse the most perfect home possible?"

Gabriel stops. Words keep wanting to spill out, but they are too painful. The Master turns to look at him, a deep love and understanding in His eyes.

"Yes," the Master answers, reading Gabriel's unspoken thoughts. "Even those who are My people there. Those who are faithful to Me—who cherish Me and keep My commandments. Even those who tell the world I am coming back for them and who pray for My return. Even those, when they begin to sense I am going to return so soon for them . . ." The Master pauses, tears filling His eyes. "They all hesitate, as if . . ." The Master cannot continue.

Gabriel turns, knowing what his Master can scarcely bring Himself to say. Gabriel faces the beauty about him, but he doesn't see it. Instead, his heart goes back to the pain of seeing the Master he loves crushed beneath the indifference and resistance shown Him by the very people He longs for. Tears in his eyes, the angel turns to his Master and takes the scarred hands in his.

"Jesus," he says.

The Master's face glows on hearing the name that so intimately connects Him with His people. The tears that began filling His eyes a moment before spill out, flowing down His cheeks. The aching disappointment fills His sobs and echoes down the empty streets as He asks, "*Don't they want to come home?*" (Adapted from an unknown source.)

For your family

Why is it *you* may not want to go home?

CHAPTER

25

TRAVELING THE NARROW WAY[1]

I once had a dream—one of those dreams you just can't forget. I dreamed I was with a vast group of people—fathers, mothers, young married couples, youth, boys, girls. Part of this group, some complete families and others unaccompanied by relatives, started on a long trip. It was more than just a vacation. It was as if the whole group had decided to move everything they had to a new home, some place we all figured was a better place to live. We packed up all our things in comfortable campers and motor homes. Everyone was quite heavily loaded—some even pulled trailers behind, loaded with supplies and personal possessions.

Everything went well at first. The roads were smooth and clear; our family sang together as we rode along. We journeyed closer and closer to a great mountain range. The closer we came, the higher the mountains loomed, and we began to wonder what was going to happen there, for our trip route took us right through the mountains. There was no other way to go. Finally, we reached the mountains, and the highway started winding up the switchbacks. The road snaked along the rim of a deep canyon. I looked over and saw nothing but empty space vanishing into darkness below.

The road grew narrower and steeper. Motors began over-heating—trucks were all in compound low, laboring and whining, struggling up the steep grade. We stopped for a moment at a roadside park, and several said they hadn't expected the road to be so difficult. The family right behind us had gotten into a serious disagreement. The wife said she had had enough—the husband wanted to go on. The children weren't sure what they wanted to do. They finally turned back in order to please the wife. The rest of us lightened the loads on our campers, trucks, and motor homes, put our excess belongings into several trailers that were left by the road, and traveled on.

The road grew even narrower. At times it seemed one of the back duals was practically hanging over the precipice. We finally held a council and decided the campers and motor homes would have to be abandoned. We unhooked our Hondas and Yamahas, sorted out our most needed possessions, put them in our backpacks, and started up the steep road again. For quite a distance the road was fine for our bikes, but gradually it became a trail about a foot wide with an occasional spot of loose gravel. Tires spun, kicking gravel off over the edge into the yawning chasm below. Nerves and muscles grew tense with the emotional strain of fighting to stay on the treacherous trail. Suddenly, our oldest son, who was on the lead cycle, skidded to a halt, and the rest of us also stopped. We walked on ahead to investigate. We found that the white granite canyon wall was getting higher and higher on our right but the path was getting so narrow that the handlebars of our bikes were beginning to rub against the walls, threatening to bounce our cycles over the precipice on the left. We held a family council and decided to leave the cycles and go on with just our backpacks. At that point, some of the church youth said they would rather go back than part with their Hondas and Yamahas. One of the group tried to turn his bike around on the narrow pathway. Two of us tried to reach out and catch him, but he kept holding onto the cycle, and we could not pull him back to the pathway. His foot slipped, and he fell over the edge of the pathway into the deep canyon below. Several of the returning group became enraged, saying they were going to notify the authorities when they got back. A brother and sister from one family refused to turn back, and we asked them to join us and sort of belong to our family.

The majority of the original group had abandoned the journey by now, but those of us who remained became even more determined to go on and complete the trip we had started out on. We all felt a strong, compelling necessity to continue. By this time we expected the trail to get harder. It did. Just when the going got very rough and the pathway we walked on became very small, little cords were let down from the top of the granite wall. We noticed that the cords traveled with us as we labored up the narrow path. We clutched these cords, small as they were, using them to help us keep our balance as we climbed. After a while, we found the pathway was so narrow our backpacks began to press against the wall and sway us out toward the abyss below. When the children saw Dad and me loosening our pack straps, they did the same—we watched our most precious possessions fall into the darkness below our path. All we had left were our clothes, a few things in our pockets, and, of course, our hiking boots.

As we edged our way along the pathway, I wondered why no one was complaining. But as I looked back down the line of people, I saw that all the complainers had long since turned back. Then the pathway suddenly became even narrower. There was hardly anywhere now to place our feet. Our whole weight had to be suspended from the cords, which had grown larger as we had progressed up the pathway. Finally, we found that even our hiking boots were giving us trouble. They were too thick to feel the pathway accurately. First one and then the other of us loosened the lacings of our boots and let them fall away, feeling our way along the pathway with the bare soles of our feet. Our feet weren't used to such treatment and became bruised and finally began to bleed from small cuts. Somehow this made us even more determined to go on. We could see from blood marks on the pathway and wall that others had gone this way before us, and this gave us courage to go on. I remember thinking how encouraging it would be for those who came after us on the pathway to see the bloodstains from our family's feet. It would give them courage to keep on to the end.

The path now became so narrow we could get only a portion of our feet on the pathway. We had to edge along the wall, putting all our weight on the cords, which seemed to be getting larger at each step. As we suspended more and more of our weight on the cords, Dad exclaimed, "We're being held from above!" Down the line, Mom, the children, and other exhausted travelers passed the word, "We're being held from above! We're being held from above!"

Down below us, in the darkness, we could see dimly flashing lights. Sounds of music, parties, and revelry drifted up from the blackness. We kept moving. We couldn't see how the pathway could get any narrower, but it did. Finally we came to the end. The path ended on a ledge just big enough for us all to stand on. But beyond the end of the pathway was nothing but a great chasm, and there was nothing but darkness down below. What were we to do now? There was no longer any pathway to guide our feet. The only thing we had to depend on were the cords. They were no longer small. Instead, they had grown until they were as big as our bodies. Now the terrible question was passed down the line: "To what are the cords attached? Can we be sure of them?"

My husband was just ahead of me and the children just behind. I could see the sweat running down his forehead in large drops. The veins in his neck were twice as large as usual as he stood in anguish, trying to decide what to do, trying to decide if he could put his trust in the cords. I could feel the sweat running in streams down my face and back. The children were in anguish. A fearful struggle was before

210

us. Should we fail here, all the difficulties of our journey would have been experienced for nothing.

In front of us, on the other side of the chasm, was a beautiful field of green grass about six inches high. I could not see the sun, but soft beams of light lighted up the field. The sunbeams looked like gold and silver as they rested on it. Nothing I had ever seen on earth could compare with the beauty and glory of this field. But there was still the question—could we succeed in getting across that awful chasm and in reaching the other side? Could we make it? The pressure of the question was terrible. If the cord should break, we would perish.

Again, words of anguish were whispered: "What holds the cord?" For a moment we hesitated to venture. Then suddenly we exclaimed, "Our only hope is to trust wholly to the cord. It has been our support all this difficult way. It will not fail us now . . ." But still, some of our friends were hesitant and distressed. Then the words were spoken, "God holds the cord. We need not fear." These words were repeated by those who stood behind us, and they added, "He will not fail us now. He has brought us thus far in safety."

My husband took hold of the cord and swung himself over into the beautiful field beyond the chasm. I immediately followed—and the children a few moments later. And oh, what a sense of relief and gratitude to God flooded our hearts and minds. We gathered in our unbroken family circle, including the other boy and his sister whom we had adopted when their own family had turned back. We raised our voices in triumphant praise to God. I was happy—perfectly happy! We had gone through together—through crisis to victory!

---

1. A paraphrase of *Life Sketches*, 190-193, prepared by John B. Youngberg and Winston Ferris.

CHAPTER

26

HOME AT LAST!

The family was having their worship on Sabbath evening, and the topic of discussion was the heavenly home. The father asks little Jenny, "How can we get ready for Jesus to come?" She thinks for a few moments and then runs off to another room and returns, pulling on an open suitcase.

"What are you doing?" he asks as she gently steps into the suitcase.

"I am getting ready for Jesus to take me to heaven in my suitcase. I'm just packing my suitcase with *me*." That was Jenny's idea of how she was going to get to her heavenly home.

While selling Christian books a number of years ago, I came to a little shack of a home. A disabled man came to the door and invited me into his humble dwelling. Inside were two of his brothers, both disabled in some way, either physically or emotionally. There were muscle problems, and one was blind. There were deformities of all kinds—a sad scene of humanity and poverty. My heart was pained at the sight of these crippled, relatively young men. I left with a heavy heart and a deep desire for Christ to come and restore this earth to what God had intended it to be—a place with no more poverty, pain, emotional hurts, crying, or death. There is a better home for all of us, and I long for it. Don't you?

Some of our homes may be lovely, some simple and comfortable, but others are not adequate at all. Then there are the homeless. No matter what kind of home we might have, our final home will far surpass anything that we could ever have on this earth. Let us pray that we will soon take up residence in that better land, where a mansion has already been prepared for us.

It was different with Christ than with us. He had a glorious home but chose to abandon it for poverty, self-sacrifice, humiliation, and ultimately a cruel death, in order that humanity might be saved and have eternal life. Many times Jesus had no place to lay his head—with the disciples, He would sleep out in the open on the Mount of Olives.

Have you ever thought what the home of Jesus was like before He left it to descend to earth? The royal Kingdom of God, the local address of Jesus, where He sat at the right hand of God, must have been magnificent, glorious, dazzling with splendor, majestic. It was a royal residence for a regal potentate—Jesus. Holy angels waited on His command. There was continuous music as angels sang in infinitely melodious harmony, "Holy, Holy, Holy." They worshiped Him with deep love and awed respect. The beauty all around Him—with gold, silver, and a sea of glass—is beyond any earthly imagination.

All was perfect in heaven until Lucifer, one of the covering cherubs, became jealous of Christ, and rebellion took place in that perfect, heavenly home. Lucifer said it was impossible to keep the commandments of God—they were arbitrary and unjust. He claimed the right to be equal with God and proposed to take authority by force if necessary. There was war in heaven. The peace was shattered by armies of angels. God cast Lucifer and his rebel angels to earth, leaving millions and millions of vacant places in the kingdom.

God could have destroyed Lucifer and his angels as easily as you can snap your finger. But to blot out the rebels would have left questions in the minds of unfallen beings. Lucifer claimed he could run a better government, and God determined to give him a fair chance to demonstrate his principles. And thus came the story of how the devil in the form of a snake tempted Adam and Eve to sin. The sentence of death was pronounced on humankind.

The only possible solution to this cosmic problem was for Jesus to put aside His royal privileges in His heavenly home of grandeur and cover His divinity with humanity. He gave up His honor and all the riches of heaven to become poor for those He loved. Jesus came to this world of darkness to suffer persecution and, ultimately, a shameful death, that we might have a home with Him. "God so loved the world, that he gave his only begotten Son, that whosoever believeth in him should not perish, but have everlasting life." He ransomed us—He paid the price.

Because Jesus has promised to put an end to the conflict between good and evil so that His chosen family can go home where they belong, He has started orchestrating the battle's concluding events. Seeing all the deprivation and suffering caused by sin, Jesus longs to bring about change and desires to establish us in our new residence soon. He yearns to get us out of this earthly confusion and our perplexing lives. He has a better home and lifestyle in store for us in the Promised Land. That is why Jesus has begun to make travel arrangements for those who love Him and choose to keep His commandments.

The arrangements are about finished. Soon the glorious transfer from earth to heaven will take place. Of course, there will be some adjustments as to who will really be able to make the trip. There will be hardships before the journey starts, to verify who really wants to go. Ultimately, we each make the choice.

Home at Last!

Imagine with me what the journey will be like. Christ will personally come to pick us up and will bring all the angels of heaven with Him, since He wants this trip to the new home to never, ever, be forgotten by any of us or the heavenly beings.

Cousin Millie used to come to get me in an old Model A. But Jesus, the King of kings, will provide an enormous spacecraft for our journey home. It will come from the East like an immense, dazzling, and glorious cloud. At a distance of thousands of miles, it may look at first like a small dark cloud, but then it will become a towering one with a brilliant rainbow over it. Under the cloud will appear what looks like flaming fire. Let's imagine the scene as if we are there.

Jesus comes triumphantly in all glory and splendor, with the brilliance of thousands and thousands and thousands of radiant angels in their white robes. They escort Him in this "Welcome Home" entourage. Luminous and brighter than spotless white, our King will wear a robe—and victorious golden crowns within crowns rest on His hair. He comes as a joyous, excited bridegroom to meet those He loves so dearly. His eyes are like penetrating fire. He holds a silver trumpet in His left hand and a sharp cutting sickle in His right. The Son of Man, the Saviour of the world, comes majestically now as the King of kings and the Lord of lords. The homeward journey is about to begin. I can hardly wait for this exciting moment.

Those who do not know Jesus as their beloved King, however, have pale faces and fear in their hearts. For a moment, the angels stop singing, and everything becomes painfully quiet. Then Jesus speaks. The Mighty One says, "Those who have clean hands and pure hearts will be able to join us for the journey home." Splendid mansions in the New Jerusalem await those who have washed their robes and made them white in the blood of the Lamb.

UNBROKEN CIRCLE

Before the actual journey takes place, some unfinished business on earth must be cared for. Those who died with a deep love of Jesus will be resurrected at the reverberating sound of Jesus' silver trumpet. The great trumpet call goes to the north, south, east, and west. In a mighty voice, Jesus calls out to those who still sleep in their graves, "Awake! Awake! Awake! Ye that sleep in the dust, and arise!" With a mighty earthquake beyond measure on the Richter Scale, the earth heaves, and the dead in Christ come triumphantly from their graves. Alleluias and praise ring throughout the earth.

My mother and Cousin Millie, Grandma and Grandpa Youngberg, Bonnie (John's first wife, who died of a brain tumor), and so many loved ones and friends are clothed in immortality and are taken up into the air to meet the waiting Jesus and His party of rejoicing and praising angels. The babies who had died on earth are put into the arms of their mothers by the children's guardian angels. There are tears of joy at this great emotional moment of reunion. Alleluia! We are all going home together as a family.

Those who are alive are released from their mountain hiding places, and the prison doors are opened. The exiled are caught up by the angels from the lonely spots. Joining those raised from the dead with hugs and kisses of joy, the celebration begins.

It takes us a week to travel to our new residence. During this time there is silence in heaven, because all the angels are in Christ's entourage. They want to be part of this once-only journey of the redeemed. We will stop off at different worlds on the way. Since the trip takes seven days, all have kept at least one Sabbath before arriving in heaven.

At the sea of glass, there is more celebration. Jesus Himself places the golden crowns on our heads (and they're the right size!). Other welcome-home gifts include harps of gold and palms of victory. All are happy with their crowns, though

Home at Last!

some are heavy with stars and some have few. Regal white robes are given to each in preparation for the march over the sea of glass to the gates of the city. Jesus leads the way. He swings open the gates of pearl and tells us that we have stood for the truth and have been cleansed by His blood. He says, "Welcome home. Enter in."

"Alleluia!" we sing out together in a massive choir—and we cross the threshold.

Finally we, the redeemed, are at our new home, and we feel that we have a perfect right to be there. We gaze upon the tree of life and the throne of Jehovah God. What a majestic and glorious scene. In praise we stroke our harps, and all heaven rings with adoration as every creature joins in grateful thanksgiving to the Almighty God, the Son Jesus, and the Holy Spirit.

The time has come for the Agape Feast. Jesus' invitation is extended for all the redeemed to come to the banquet table, and He Himself serves us. The table of silver is miles long, but we can all see each other. It is covered with "fruit of the tree of life, manna, almonds, figs, pomegranates, grapes, and many other kinds of fruit." And we don't have to pay an expensive banquet fee to partake. It is free.

After a short thousand years, there is another trip when we, the redeemed, come back to the earth with the angels. Christ descends upon the Mount of Olives. The great city of God, the New Jerusalem, comes down from heaven in brilliant splendor, prepared as a bride adorned for her husband.

The long-awaited end of seven thousand years of sin has come. The final coronation of Jesus, the Son of God, the Saviour of the lost human race, as King of kings and Lord of lords takes place with dignity and majesty. "Worthy! Worthy is the Lamb!" we sing. Jesus the Victor sits on His throne. The books are opened, and a panoramic video of the great controversy is projected on the screen of the sky, that all may know that God is just.

One more battle is fought between good and evil, but, praise God, Satan's time is up. The enemy is defeated for the last time. We wave palm branches in victory. Cleansing fire comes down, and the earth is purified for the children of God. No more temptations. No more trials. No more pain. There is a new heaven and a new earth. The old has been taken away. (See Revelation 21:1.)

The saved in chorus declare, " 'Great and marvelous are Your works, Lord God Almighty! Just and true are Your ways, O King of the saints!' " (Revelation 15:3, NKJV). And we fall on our knees in adoration and worship the majestic King of kings.

When some of the celebrations are over, you and I have time to look around. We see beautiful houses that appear to be made of silver and pearl. Inside, they have a golden shelf on which we put our glittering crowns. Outside, we view gorgeous flowers—roses, lilies, tulips, bougainvillea, and all kinds of perfect blooms with exquisite petals of delicate and brilliant rainbow colors that perfume the air. There are meadows of living, vibrant, green grass having a reflection of gold and silver.

As we further explore our new environment, we find the animals and beasts of the field we once feared all peacefully grazing together in the meadows. I think now of the time when friends who liked to feed wild animals turned a spotlight on in their backyard for us to see their animal friends. There, side by side, were raccoon, skunk, and opossum eating together, not disturbed in the least by each other. The lion, the lamb, the wolf, the leopard, plus the cheetah, the antelope, and every imaginable beast of the field will be at peace with each other and with us. What an open space zoo, with no fences and no fees!

On the way to Mount Zion, we walk through the woods and feel safe. Some of the children wing their way toward the heights. Presently, we see some young and some older ones who have red borders on the hems of their white robes. These are those who were martyred for the cause of God's kingdom. They, too, make their way to Mt. Zion.

After getting acquainted with our new environment, we join in the heavenly school with an infinite number of things to occupy our time and keep us active. We study into what really happened at Creation as well as the historical events of the world. Everything is made perfectly clear. We hear the music of nature not heard before. We sing the song of Moses and the Lamb with unending joy.

We listen enthralled to the stories of angels, who tell us how they protected us time and time again. Our guardian angels tell us of how they intervened in our spiritual journey. We are told how we helped others heavenward and exchange stories of victory in the great controversy between good and evil. We hold sweet communion at our own home place with honored guests like Peter, Paul, Adam, Ruth, Esther, Isaiah, Timothy, Mary (the mother of Jesus), Eve, Elijah and all the great and small in heaven's Hall of the Redeemed.

There are no limitations to the activities in our new home with Christ and the saints of all ages. Never do we hear, "This is boring." Each day, at home or away, new and exciting adventures unfold throughout eternity. Let's be there! Please look us up. Check with Zion's Information Center to find our local address so you will have no trouble finding us.

And—oh yes—we can join each other as we travel to other worlds. I understand they want to hear our story of what it was like on planet Earth during the last thrilling days of the great controversy. Most of all, they never tire of hearing how Jesus came to our rescue. We can share our stories, OK?

Isaiah tells us (65:21, 22, KJV), "They shall build houses, and inhabit them; and they shall plant vineyards, and eat the fruit of them. They shall not build, and another inhabit; they shall not plant, and another eat: for as the days of a tree are the days of my people, and mine elect shall long enjoy the work of their hands." We may not be accomplished carpenters on this earth, but in the earth made new, skills will be given us so that our home will be the result of our creative imagination and desires.

Besides all the beauty and blessings, there is no more pain or hurt, no more hunger or thirst, no more sweltering heat or floods to wipe away our homes, no more fear or crying or death. These are all gone, never to be remembered again. You and I live on new planet Earth in perfect harmony forever and ever, and it isn't just a fairy tale story, but it is *for real* for you, for me, and for our family who love Jesus and keep His commandments. Best of all—Jesus is there and His holy beauty fills us with such great love. Our hearts burst into grateful praise as we sing, "Holy, Holy, Holy."

Today Jesus stretches out His hands to you. Look at the scars where the spikes pierced them and recall the agony at Gethsemane. And He says, "I did all this so you and your family could come home with me."

In the Bible the inheritance of the saved is called "a country." . . . There the heavenly Shepherd leads His flock to fountains of living waters. The tree of life yields its fruit every month, and the leaves of the tree are for the service of the nations. There are ever-flowing streams, clear as crystal, and beside them waving trees cast their shadows upon the paths prepared for the ransomed of the Lord. There the wide-spreading plains swell into hills of beauty, and the mountains of God rear their lofty summits. On those peaceful plains, beside those living streams, God's people, so long pilgrims and wanderers, shall find a home (*The Great Controversy*, 675).

Just a few more days, and our earthly wanderings will be

finished. Let's all be ready. Jesus invites you, along with your family. May your circle be unbroken forever!

God is giving you another invitation. Even if this life has not been in harmony with heavenly living, He still extends an invitation.

For your family

1. Please read the following quote as a family. What does the last sentence say to your family? If there are small children in the family, have them draw a picture of Jesus giving them their crowns, while parents watch. Place the drawings in some special spot for all to see for a week.

With joy unutterable, parents see the crown, the robe, the harp, given to their children. The days of hope and fear are ended. The seed sown with tears and prayers may have seemed to be sown in vain, but their harvest is reaped with joy at last. Their children have been redeemed. Fathers, mothers, shall the voices of your children swell the song of gladness in that day? (*Child Guidance*, 569).

2. Have the children continue to draw pictures of what they think the "welcome home" scene will look like, so that it will be more visually fixed in their minds. Help them form their own images and ideas—let them be as creative as they wish. To help them with the picture, read to them about heaven from some of Ellen White's books.

3. Older members of the family—do your own personal study about going home to heaven and the events that will take place on the homeward journey. Share with someone or at some church function.

4. What plans do you personally have about going home? What plans do you have for your family about going home? Is every family member included?

UNBROKEN CIRCLE

Some years ago, a gentleman from the Caribbean came to our home one evening. We invited him in, and for a few minutes we chatted about this and that. The thought occurred to us that probably he had some family problem he wanted to talk about. After a while, he got around to the topic of his visit and shared with us that as he had studied about the "Elijah message" of family heart-turning, God had impressed him he should do something for the various members of his family. It was his deep desire that all his numerous family would go home to heaven together. He was making plans to go the coming weekend to Toronto and had already alerted the whole family there to be together, as he had important things to share with them. He called on us for additional material for his presentation. We supplied him with available studies and strategies on this subject, prayed with him, and sent him off on this mission of love.

He returned from Toronto exuberant and shared with us how God had sent conviction on those who had gathered and that there was a spirit of healing and oneness among them. Then he continued, "I also have family in New York. Now I'm going there to share this heart-turning message with them." He arrived in New York on Friday evening and soon lost his way. He knew he was close to the address, but among all the high-rises, he wasn't just sure which apartment building was the right one. As he waited in the street asking God to direct his way, he heard the strands of "Day Is Dying in the West" coming from one of the apartments. He made his way to this location and knocked on the door. He found a Seventh-day Adventist family in Friday evening worship. By further inquiry, he learned that although his relatives lived in the same apartment complex, these families did not know each other. There was a cementing of relationships with this branch of the family. He put them in contact with their believing neighbors and rejoiced to see that heart-turning was taking place.

Home at Last!

And still the story wasn't finished. Next, this brother thought of his childhood home in Jamaica, and some weeks later he flew there with the urgent message that the King is coming and that his greatest desire was to see all of his loved ones going home together.

Could your family plan some family get-togethers where any misunderstandings of the past could be put away and in heart-turning you could encourage one another to turn your steps toward home? What decision will you make about sharing with your own kith and kin the good news that Jesus is returning soon to take them home, to take your entire family circle home if each one wishes to go?

References

This chapter is based in part on the following references. Spend more time reading and discussing these references.

Matthew 24

The Desire of Ages, 739

The Youth's Instructor, 5 September 1895

Education, 301-309

Early Writings, 15-20

The Great Controversy, 299, 648, 662-678

Lift Him Up, 207

"Reasons for Having Courage," *Advent Review and Sabbath Herald*, 29 July 1890, *Colporteur Ministry*, 110

"Be Diligent," *Signs of the Times*, 10 February 1988

"In Gethsemane," *Signs of the Times*, 9 December 1987

The Upward Look, 104

Isaiah 62:5

To contact the Youngbergs for speaking engagements or information, write or call

Family Life International
Andrews University
Berrien Springs, MI 49104
(616) 471-6366